Resources of Music

Living School Music

RESOURCES OF MUSIC
General Editor: John Paynter

Books for the Classroom

Cantors by Mary Berry
Minstrels 2 by Brian Sargent
Poverty Knock by Roy Palmer
Something to Play by Geoffrey Brace
Strike the Bell by Roy Palmer
The Painful Plough by Roy Palmer
The Rigs of the Fair by Roy Palmer and Jon Raven
The Valiant Sailor by Roy Palmer
Troubadours by Brian Sargent
Troubadours and Minstrels, record (Brian Sargent)

Books for Teachers

Electronic Music for Schools by Richard Orton
Folk Music in School edited by Robert Leach and Roy Palmer
Jazz by Graham Collier
Jazz: Illustrations, record (Graham Collier)
Jazz: Lecture Concert, record (Graham Collier)
Pop Music in School (New Edition) edited by Graham Vulliamy and Ed Lee
Pop Music in School: Illustrations, cassette (Graham Vulliamy and Ed Lee)
Pop, Rock and Ethnic Music in School edited by Graham Vulliamy and Ed Lee
Sound and Silence by John Paynter and Peter Aston
Sound and Silence, record (John Paynter and Peter Aston)
Vibrations by David Sawyer

LIVING SCHOOL MUSIC

WILLIAM SALAMAN

Department of Education, University College, Cardiff

CAMBRIDGE UNIVERSITY PRESS
Cambridge
London   New York   New Rochelle
Melbourne   Sydney

Published by the Press Syndicate of the University of Cambridge
The Pitt Building, Trumpington Street, Cambridge CB2 1RP
32 East 57th Street, New York, NY 10022, USA
296 Beaconsfield Parade, Middle Park, Melbourne 3206, Australia

First published 1983

Printed in Great Britain at the University Press, Cambridge

Library of Congress catalogue card number: 83–10092

British Library cataloguing in publication data
Salaman, William
  Living school music–(Resources of music)
  1. School music–Instruction and study
  I. Title II. Series
  780'.72 MT1

  ISBN 0 521 25453 1 hard covers
  ISBN 0 521 27472 9 paperback

Thanks are due to the following for permission to reproduce material in their copyright:
Chapter 4, Southern Music Publishing Co. Ltd
Chapter 5, © 1977 Middle Eight Music Ltd, 99 St Martin's Lane, London WC2N 4AZ

CONTENTS

To Clare, Rachel and Anna

ACKNOWLEDGEMENTS

I am tremendously grateful to many kind colleagues, friends and relations who have taken the trouble to read the manuscript of this book and who have made suggestions for its improvement.

I thank most warmly David Allsobrook, David Fontana, Grenville Hancox, Goronwy Jones, John Paynter, Esther Salaman, Piers Spencer and Keith Swanwick for their encouragement and detailed criticisms. I have been cheered on by many others and most of all by my wife who has given me her consistent and invaluable support.

William Salaman

1 INTRODUCTION

Music education is an excitingly diverse subject. The quantity and variety of the activities and ideas available might remind us of the giant menus which are thrust into our hands in certain restaurants. We peruse the catalogue of dishes, vacillate for a while and finally opt for the one which is safe and familiar, perhaps feeling a twinge of regret at our timidity. Similarly, in music education, we might examine the books on our shelf and notice how huge is the range of offerings: singing; recorder playing; Orff-Schulwerk; creative music-making; harmony and counterpoint; percussion band; musical theory; teaching for examinations; integration of the arts; music for slow learners and more.

Most of these books concern themselves with method, means or idiom. Celebrated schemes of work such as those of Orff, Curwen and Kodály form the core of the method section, though other books lean in that direction, especially if we think of the word 'method' as embracing specific approaches like creative music-making and performing from grid notations. The means for making music are generally voices and instruments. In this section we find books on vocal training and the uses of instruments in the classroom, though again there are more recent additions including work with synthesisers, tape recorders and electronic keyboards. Looking further along the shelf, we come to the idiom section. Here stand books on the uses of rock and pop, medieval music, avant-garde possibilities and the like.

The book you are reading now is not principally about method, means or idiom. Its main concern lies with living school music in both its senses: living the life of a school music teacher and working to create an environment within the classroom for the music itself to live.

As a music teacher working in a secondary school, I found myself playing two rôles: one as a class music teacher and the other as a *Kapellmeister*. When teaching classes, I responded to the school bell like any other member of staff, turning my thoughts towards the classroom and the next lesson. As *Kapellmeister*, I organised the talented and interested pupils into choirs and orchestras and gathered audiences from time to time to witness the results. The headmaster, the parents and my colleagues appeared to value my *Kapellmeister*'s duties more highly than the other. Rarely was I asked by anyone about the classwork, yet a concert or carol service would generate kind comments and con-

1

gratulations. As the headmaster made an appropriate speech and shook my hand after a school concert, some awkward thoughts ran through my head: 'If you're so pleased by this event, why don't you employ me to mount concerts and make the classwork voluntary? . . . All hundred and fifty children taking part in this concert missed their lessons this morning in order to attend the final rehearsal. Doesn't this demonstrate that music is very important in this school? . . . I know why *I'm* pleased with this concert, but why are *you* pleased?'

I thought about this last question a good deal. I could not convince myself that the music had been enjoyed particularly. The junior brass ensemble had played alarmingly out of tune at times and the whole programme had been too heavy for most of the listeners present. I could not convince myself that the concert was a shop window. The displays in shop windows are samples of the goods which lie behind the entrance doors. No-one at the concert nursed an impression that similar music-making was pursued in my music lessons. I could not convince myself that it was recognition of 'a job of work well done'. The other teachers in the school steered their pupils through examinations and into universities. They were not applauded, nor did they have their hands shaken in public.

I think the root of the pleasure gained at the concert lay in its living quality. So much of the justification for educational practice is found in thoughts for the future. We teach business studies so that pupils can find jobs when they leave school. We teach simultaneous equations so that pupils will be equipped to understand advanced mathematical concepts later, so that they can enter university, so that they can secure a job. We teach history and geography so that the children will grow into well-informed adults, languages so that eventually they will be able to communicate in other tongues. But what about *now*? There is little in our schools which reaps immediate reward, yet this concert did. Using only voices and instruments, the children created intangible experiences for themselves and their audience. Despite its unevenness, the music rose above the humdrum rituals of today and pre-empted the promises of tomorrow.

My *Kapellmeister*'s duties were easily defined. I was expected to organise the visiting instrumental teachers' timetables, to enter instrumentalists for practical examinations, to play in assembly and to mount concerts. As a class teacher, I had to teach seemingly innumerable classes of younger children and to train a handful of older children for C.S.E., 'O' level and 'A' level examinations. As most of the examination candidates were music specialists already involved in voluntary activities, both they and I looked upon their lessons as an intrusion of *Kapellmeister* time into the normal timetabled day. The duties I owed to the three hundred children who came to me each week were much less clear. This aspect of my teaching life was not so much 'living school music' as 'living school'. It became apparent that the lessons, the children and my strategies had to fit into the routines of the school. Musical considerations would have to be placed second. Few specific instructions were given. However, it was made plain that I should write a report on each child periodically, that I had to attend meetings with parents in order to discuss their children's progress, that I would be expected to set internal examinations and keep records of achievement. The last of these presented a challenge. Should I give B+ for recorder playing and C− for listening? The idea seemed absurd, but as the first two duties arose, I realised the need for the third. When writing reports or meeting parents, I would at times search my memory in vain to recall who a particular child was. With a mark-book containing a neat row of Cs, I was able to write or say: 'Could do better.'

I found that in order to run the normal music lessons smoothly, I was obliged to bend the musical content. In contrast to this, I could play the *Kapellmeister*'s role with musical freedom. This freedom allowed the extra-curricular activities to be alive and immediate. Such life and immediacy should be made available to everyone in their normal lessons but barriers arise from within the fabric of the school's organisation and expectations. Of these, the latter must be challenged most strongly. We can cope with the organisational problems: the all-too-short single lessons, the banding and streaming, the inevitable thirty children at a time. We cannot always meet the expectations however: to produce marks and grades, to set examinations, to couch reports in conventional teacher's language, in short, to turn music into a typical school subject. These features of school life, which disturb and distort our teaching, have to be resisted. If such resistance leads to a flowering of living music, we need have no anxieties. Head teachers are inclined to support teachers who succeed − to back the horses which are already winning the race. School governors and parents tend to support head teachers, so a demonstration of successful work in the classroom should reap encouragement rather than censure.

In this book I have described some of my attempts at bringing music to life in my normal lessons. I felt that the kernel of the response to my school concert was an appreciation of music's living qualities − qualities which could be made available in normal lessons.

I found that merely wanting the music to come alive in my lessons did not necessarily cause it to happen. I had to learn how to teach and to work out for myself why I was adopting certain strategies in preference to others. This book is not presented as a blueprint for the teaching of music. It describes aspects of living classroom music which I have found useful. There are accounts of failure alongside those of success. I hope that their inclusion will bring heart to others in their search for new answers and new questions in their professional lives.

2 MATTERS OF PRINCIPLE

When, as a student, I was interviewed for entry to a post-graduate course of teacher training, I was asked the rather unfair question: 'Why do you want to teach music?' I would have liked to answer: 'I can't do anything else' or 'I want to live off a grant for another year' or 'It's the only job I can find with twelve weeks' holiday.' In fact, I said something like: 'I like music. I want to stay close to the subject' or 'I like children' or 'I was taught by an excellent teacher. I would like to teach as he did.' An answer which never occurred to me at the time was : 'I think everyone needs musical experiences and I would like to satisfy those needs.'

Probably most of us, if we can, aim to satisfy ourselves in the pursuit of our careers. I took such a view when I embarked upon professional playing and also when I began school music teaching. I seldom thought of the 'needs' of concert audiences when I played professionally or even of the 'needs' of my pupils when I taught in schools. I enjoyed the French horn and I enjoyed standing up in front of a class of children. Having made the switch to music teaching, I consulted books on the subject. I found that many of them adopted a somewhat evangelical approach towards the job. Apparently, the music teacher's task was to improve the 'taste' of the children. They should know about music, musicians, musical instruments; they should sing and play nicely; above all, they should strive to approach the imposing and immutable edifice of music as a subject and thus enter the magic world of the musical initiates. I felt a little uncomfortable about all this and without altogether knowing what I was doing, groped towards a different foundation for my music teaching.

As a student, I found it hard to relate the lectures on the philosophy of education to the realities of teaching practice. The broad purposes of education seemed entirely irrelevant to my frequent struggles with ill-disciplined, uninterested adolescents. However, once settled into a job, I found myself searching for a basis for music teaching – a basis unlike that proposed in so many of the books I read. I forced myself to question a number of assumptions and found it to be a tortuous process. I had to find a convincing rationale for *me* and I am not suggesting that the conclusions I reached are universally applicable or unchangeable.

My first question was: 'What shall I do with these children?' The actor who forgets his lines is an unenviable figure and I certainly did not wish to be seen empty-handed by the classes I taught. Songbooks were available, some of them

4

quite lively and up-to-date, and the children enjoyed singing. I worked at diction and musical precision and soon every class could sing 'The Titanic' with meticulous gusto. Notation is to music what numbers are to mathematics or vocabulary is to French. If I teach music, I thought, I must teach notation. So I did. Listening is important. I must do some listening. Beethoven is music's Shakespeare. I want to share my enthusiasm for Beethoven with these children. So it went on: recorder work, instruments of the orchestra, and bits and pieces of musical history.

Very soon I questioned these approaches. My unease stemmed from a growing realisation that my planning and decisions were based on a somewhat illogical mixture of two assumptions. One was that the children were there to serve the music, to keep it alive, to be worker bees nourishing an all-powerful queen. The other was that my aims should be related to myself. What should I do? How should I do it? If I had used student-style lesson plans at that time I might have written under the heading 'Aim': 'To teach the song "Yellow Submarine" and to instil some understanding of dotted rhythm.' The aim was all about *me*. *I* was going to teach and *I* was going to instil. The children and the music were there to give *me* something to do.

My doubts arose after I had given the lessons. I *did* teach 'Yellow Submarine' and I *did* explain the mechanics of dotted rhythm, but what then? At best, I could conclude that I was a reasonably successful teaching technician but was I really fulfilling my rôle as a music teacher? I read more books and became further confused. Some writers seemed to suggest that children should express themselves through music while others attached importance to a systematic preparation for 'O' level. To some, the music teacher should be influencing the 'inner lives' of their pupils while to others, he should be striving to teach fluency in musical literacy. The general and particular were becoming jumbled up in my mind, but at least one factor emerged with some clarity. I had to decide what the *children* needed rather than what I myself wanted to do.

In most other school subjects, it appeared that the children were being given some familiarity with the essence of each discipline so that they could feel a sense of achievement in those areas. They were not being trained as professional linguists, physicists or footballers, yet their responses to those subjects were being awakened by their being given the opportunities to experience and achieve appropriate advances at their own levels. Similarly, in music, it seemed of fundamental importance that the children should be able to acquire musical experiences and a sense of musical achievement. This became a sort of yardstick for me and helped to clear away all sorts of worries about whether to teach notation or not, whether the work should be mainly vocal or instrumental, whether it should be creative or interpretative and so on. If I could provide the children with some sort of musical experience and a sense of achievement, then I would be doing my job. Experience and achievement lie at the heart of music's appeal. The child drumming 'Chopsticks' on the piano or the legendary whistling ploughboy speak of their experience and achievement without words. The justification for music lies solely in one's involvement with it.

As a teacher, I saw my job as one of developing and heightening these intangible but nevertheless real areas of human awareness. A breakthrough, I thought, but, all too soon, a new problem arose. How could I be sure that I was promoting musical experience and achievement? I often wondered whether the children were even listening to the records I played, let alone getting any benefit from them. In a listening lesson, quiet children are not necessarily appreciative children. I realised that in order to find out the effectiveness of what I did, I would have to measure the results in some way. I went back to books for advice and this time I got more help. I learned that the educationalist tries to effect a change in his pupils. Put rather crudely, this means that a child should emerge from a lesson a little altered as a result of whatever went on in the lesson. He should know something or be able to do something or have experienced something which has changed him. This is, perhaps, the difference between education and entertainment. But we can only be sure that a change has taken place if we can measure or at least discern it. Experience and achievement are such elusive qualities, the application of normal evaluation procedures (pencil and paper tests and the like) would be ineffective. The confusion induced by all these thoughts encouraged me to put the problem on paper:

I must define the children's musical needs.
Broadly speaking, these needs are for musical experience and achievement.
How do I know whether the needs are being met by the course of work I offer?
By measuring the results.
How?
I don't know.

The second breakthrough occurred when I released my thoughts from music alone and tried to envisage parallel issues elsewhere. Many examples presented themselves. For instance, a government might have the overall aim of 'bettering the community's welfare'. It introduces a tax cut. The effects of this cut can be measured only in figures relating to the wealth of individuals. Whether it 'betters the community's welfare' or not is almost impossible to discern. The tax cut represents only a small part of an overall strategy.

Most parents would wish to do the 'best' for their children, to help them grow into happy, responsible adults. Their choice of birthday present may help in a small way towards this end, but again, their success or failure cannot be measured in such terms.

Aims: general and particular

The implications for music education became obvious. I can measure the change that takes place in the children during one music lesson but I should not try to do so in terms of the overall aim. In other words, the goals of experience and achievement apply to the course as a whole, not to every small part. The goals for a single lesson should be much more precise. If I can add together all the positive results of many lessons, I should find myself with evidence, proof almost, that the overall aim is being met. I might decide that recorder playing from written notation is an activity which serves the main aim of my course: that is, it contributes towards musical experience and achievement. So, an early recorder lesson might concentrate on the fingerings and notation for the notes B, A and G. Clearly, the aim of the lesson has nothing to do with experience and achievement in a direct way. The aim is small and specific and could be phrased like this:

Aim: By the end of the lesson the children will be able to read and play on recorders the notes B, A and G.

I can measure easily whether the aim has been met or not. If the children can read and play as intended then they have done the musical equivalent of getting a sum right in mathematics. A series of successes will contribute towards the fulfilment of the central aim.

I reduced these thoughts to a maxim for myself: The aims of the *course* are general in nature and do not vary. The aims of the *lessons* are precise and vary a great deal.

So I worked in this way, selecting those activities which I thought met the main aims of my course and then devised measurable objectives for each lesson. (I have never been able to discern a semantic difference between the words 'aim' and 'objective'. My own uses of the words will be explained carefully later in this chapter.) In reality, only rarely did I actually measure. I simply got into the habit of asking myself if the objective of a given lesson had been met or not. It was obvious enough whether the children could play and/or read a new note, whether they could sing a certain interval with precision, whether they could follow a score. However, some activities *were* tested: aural work, writing notation into books and so on.

I continued to work along these lines until further doubts arose. The everyday work in the classroom was becoming too haphazard. It lacked direction. I could find no good reason for doing one activity rather than another and I began to worry lest the musical needs of the children, as I saw them, were not being met because of some invisible shortcoming in planning or method. I wondered whether I had narrowed down too finely the areas of work within music. Should I be more creative in my approach? Should I be using jazz and rock idioms in the classroom? Should I be integrating my work with the drama department? They were nagging questions. I needed reasons for pursuing one activity rather than another in any particular lesson. Once again, pencil and paper were pressed into use.

I have two sorts of aim: One is a general aim for the course as a whole while the other is an aim for a single lesson.

The achievement of the lesson aim must be measurable or discernible.

The sum of successfully met small aims fulfils the larger aim.

What criteria do I use to decide upon the selection of small aims?
I must simply assure myself that they contribute towards the main aim.
But lots of activities do that. I haven't the time or expertise to cover everything.
Then select.
On what basis?
I don't know.

This seemed to point towards the necessity for yet another aim – a sort of middle aim. There are areas of musical experience which should be covered. I needed to list them and make sure that all were attended to during the course so that I knew that a comprehensive education in music was being offered and that I had an educational reason for opting for any particular activity. The areas in question might be listed as follows:

Vocal technique and repertoire
Instrumental technique and repertoire
Musical literacy
Creative work
Listening skills

I now asked myself this question before planning any lesson: 'In which area are my pupils in need of development?' The answer to the question formed the 'objective' for the lesson. If I felt that the children needed to improve their vocal techniques, then such improvement would become the objective for my lesson. If I felt that they should extend their listening skills, then that would become the objective. The objectives located the area or areas of musical activity in which the work would take place. What had hitherto been my 'aim' became now a stepping-stone towards the objective. Certain songs used in certain ways would help to meet the objective of improved vocal technique. A particular choice of score would serve to improve score-reading techniques and hence listening skills. Such steps have been called 'enabling objectives' by educational theorists. Though I am reluctant to use jargon and pat phrases, I feel that in this case, 'enabling objective' does describe well the purpose which underpins the activities of a single lesson. We might imagine a staircase at the top of which stands 'instrumental technique'. Just as, physically, we are unable to ascend an entire flight of stairs in a single leap, so educationally, we have to climb step by step. Each step enables us to get nearer to our ultimate objective.

I started to plan my lessons in terms of the general area for improvement (this formed the objective for the lesson) and the means or steps I would take in order to work towards the fulfilment of the objective (this formed the enabling objective for the lesson). In both cases I framed the objectives in terms of what the *children* might achieve. For example:

Objective: By the end of the lesson the children will have widened their repertoire of songs and will have extended their knowledge of rhythmic symbols.
Enabling Objective: By the end of the lesson the children will have learned the

words and music for 'Apusskidu' and will be able to read and understand the notation for a semibreve. (The semibreve features in 'Apusskidu'. Other notes used are minim and crotchet – note values covered in previous lessons.)

It can be seen that meeting the enabling objective successfully automatically *enables* the objective to be fulfilled. In my record I can note that I have covered a little work in Area 1 (vocal technique and repertoire) and Area 3 (musical literacy). Below is a summary of the pattern of objectives which I had decided to adopt for my teaching.

Overall aim for the course (This does not vary)
The children will gain musical experiences and a sense of musical achievement.
Objectives
These are the main areas of musical education which should be covered in order to fulfil the overall aim:
Vocal work, instrumental work, literacy, creative work, listening.
Enabling Objectives
These should be as specific as possible and should be measurable or discernible. They enable the children to fulfil the objectives listed above. Examples are: to master a certain instrumental skill; to understand a new rhythm; to create a convincing composition using a limited range of sound sources; to follow a score; to sing a given interval; to be able to differentiate between varying musical styles.

With experience, I found that I had no need to make lesson plans on paper. Having grasped the principles above, I simply said to myself something like: 'The children need more practice in creative music-making. In order to achieve this they will work in groups at a narrative piece using body and vocal sounds only.' Transcribed into the objectives of a formal lesson plan:

Objective: By the end of the lesson the children will have developed their capacity to work creatively in groups, using limited means.
Enabling objective: By the end of the lesson the children will have constructed a composition entitled 'The Supernatural' using body and vocal sounds only. They will work in groups of five.

Notice how the objective merely defines the area of work whereas the enabling objective is specific and is, to a certain extent, capable of being assessed.

In later chapters I will use this pattern of lesson presentation for some of the methodologies described.

The gap between a simple enabling objective and an overall aim for a course is enormous. It appeared to me that I had sorted out my thoughts on music education in a sufficiently comprehensive manner to allow me to design a single lesson on one hand or a whole year's syllabus on the other with confidence. I was wrong. I gradually became aware that some activities in class 'worked' while others did not. I examined the situation and realised that all of the objectives of my course needed guidelines, sometimes described as parameters.

The need for guidelines

The objectives can be viewed as a hierarchy, a vertical thought process leading from the enabling objectives at the bottom to the goals of musical experience and achievement at the top. What I needed were lateral boundaries. I could decide upon the suitability of an objective in the light of its effectiveness in satisfying the needs of the objective above, but I needed some reliable guidance for arriving at objectives at *any* level. I needed the comfort of a 'containing wall' so that I knew that whatever I was doing in class, it lay inside that containing wall and was therefore automatically worthwhile. With activities I had tried, my confidence in the worth or otherwise of the work had been based on observation of the children's reactions. My concern lay in the areas I had *not* tried. I was working in schools during an explosive period of music education, a period when new ideas were being put forward in great profusion. Creative music-making was becoming well known, ideas for the use of tape recorders and synthesisers were being aired. The integration of the arts in schools, pop and rock idioms, medieval music, avant-garde music, Orff-Schulwerk, project work: all these were being thrust at me in books, articles and pamphlets, at conferences and through casual conversation. They did not necessarily mix with one another and they by no means all matched my own talents as a music teacher. I badly needed a means of deciding whether it was even worth trying out some of these practices.

The three lessons outlined below might serve to illustrate my dilemma.

The first is a lesson involving invention and experiment. The children are given a free choice of all the instruments available and are instructed to create a descriptive piece of music. Almost certainly, the result must promote musical experience and a sense of achievement. The enabling objectives will relate to the choice of sounds and decisions about form etc.

The second lesson concerns the teaching of rhythmic relationships. The children will learn about the logic which underlies rhythmic notation and they will enter a clearly understood diagram of note values into their exercise books. The musical knowledge gained could be defined justifiably as an achievement and the enabling objectives will be devised in relation to the acquisition of facts.

The third is a recorder lesson based on the well-tried *School Recorder Book 1* by Priestley and Fowler. The tune to be learned is 'Loch Lomond' on page 27. Again, the children will make obvious gains in musical experience and achievement and the enabling objectives will relate to recorder fingerings and the learning of notation.

There is, however, something missing from each of these lessons. In order to find out exactly what the missing elements are, I will return to the 'boundaries' mentioned earlier. However, I will abandon the word 'boundaries' and use the word 'principles' instead. It is a more positive way of thinking about containing walls.

Three guiding principles

The three principles I arrived at emerged slowly during my school teaching career. The problems of latitude in music education reflect in some ways the problems of latitude in ordinary living. If guidelines are too stringent, imagination and enterprise are curtailed. If they are too vague, then they cannot guide and the result must be continued bewilderment.

An example of too stringent a principle might be: 'All musical activities in class must relate to the children's normal musical environment.' This implies that the work has to be based on pop and rock idioms which form the normal musical environment of most children, and that extensions of musical experience into the fields of the avant-garde or medieval music, for example, would be automatically at variance with the principle and therefore wrong. There is plenty of rewarding work to be done in pop and rock idioms, but the benefits should not be enshrined in a principle.

An example of a principle which is too vague might be: 'All activities in the music classroom must help to develop aural awareness.' It is difficult to know exactly what 'aural awareness' is. It could be quite simply an absence of deafness, or, at the other extreme, an ability to spot augmented triads and complex rhythms. Almost every activity in every school subject demands some sort of aural awareness. By making a principle of it, we offer teachers no help in deciding upon the worth of activities which might be used in class.

The word 'principle' implies an absolute standard against which behaviour can be measured. To me, my three principles are immutable but at the same time they are compromises between the extremes outlined above.

First Principle: The work must be suitable for the majority of pupils in the class

For a long time, music has been regarded by some as an élitist field, an area for the pursuit of excellence: 'The virtuosi emerge as a consequence of a long and patient process of selection, which is initiated at the average level of the many.' (G. Duhamel, 'The philosophy of music education', in *Music in Education* (U.N.E.S.C.O., 1955: International Conference on The Role and Place of Music in the Education of Youth and Adults, Brussels, 1953), pp. 23–4.) Of course, academies of music must pick the best students and strive to make them better still, but in the school music room, the teacher has no right to be selective in this way. He is no more turning out professional musicians than the art teacher is turning out professional artists or the French teacher professional linguists. If the great majority of children cannot feel involved in a musical activity because of its highly specialised nature, they will simply 'switch off' and the teacher must shoulder the blame for it.

Bearing this principle in mind, we can examine the sample lessons to see whether they abide by it or not.

The project in composition seems ideal. It demands no special techniques, involves no sophisticated concepts and must surely be manageable by most children.

The lesson on rhythmic relationships does involve concepts but of the simplest sort, comprehensible to most children of secondary age or a little younger. Every child could copy the chart into his book without trouble and most of them could grasp the intellectual aspects of the work.

The recorder lesson is the one of the three which fights the principle. 'Loch Lomond' has a range of a major ninth – low D to high E. No letter names are provided to assist in the reading and there are five different note lengths used. Only the most able and 'musical' children could tackle this tune. It would be an exceptional class of thirty children which could play genuinely from notation of this complexity. A few individuals could, no doubt, but the majority would be lost. The failure of this lesson demonstrates to me the importance of my first principle.

Second Principle: Music in the classroom should be an active, participatory subject

Of all the arts, music offers the widest scope for involvement. Any person may listen to music, any may play music and any may create music. With such a wealth of opportunity, it is surprising that music teachers have so often stressed the information aspects of the subject. A salutory reminder that attitudes do not necessarily become more enlightened with the passing of time is provided by the juxtaposition of remarks made almost two centuries apart. In 1725 in *The Musicall Gramarian* Roger North wrote:

> And grant that a man read all the books of musick that ever were wrote, I shall not allow that musick is or can be understood out of them, no more than the taste of meats out of cookish receipt books.

This spirited rejection of the passive study of music contrasts sharply with the sombre words of the anonymous writer of the Board of Education's Circular 830 of 1914, *Memoranda on Teaching and Organisation in Secondary Schools*:

> No child should be allowed to begin to play the piano till he can name notes on a large diagram of the Great Stave, in the treble and bass clefs as easily as he can read the letters of the alphabet.

It must be agreed that the Board of Education offered poor advice. The way into music is through active participation. The eloquent words of John Hullah Brown, in *Instrumental Music in Schools* (Pitman, 1938), say almost all that needs to be said on the subject:

> The earlier periods of children's musical experiences should be through the poetry of music and not the grammar of its language . . . there is a danger that many children, while able to respond to the emotional appeal, will be unable to respond to the intellectual appeal, and so, by a psychological process, come to dislike both the intellectual processes and music itself.

If musical experience and achievement are to be the goals in music education, then *activity* in its broadest sense must be a basic principle.

How do the sample lessons measure up to this principle?

The creative work certainly involves activity and participation. The making of music lies at the heart of the lesson. Similarly, the recorder lesson would be essentially active, especially if it were modified to suit the capabilities of the class being taught. But the theory lesson falls down. It may promote some sense of achievement, but it will hardly be musical achievement, and musical experience will be absent altogether. Information about music, about composers' lives and about notation is peripheral. The facts skirt the central issue of musical involvement. One might well suggest that lessons of this sort are not, in the final analysis, music lessons. The sample theory lesson is a mathematics lesson with notes substituted for numbers. Its failure again demonstrates to me the importance of my second principle.

Third principle: The activities in the music classroom should be organised into structured courses of study

The alternative to structure in music education is not anarchy or total disaster or any other headline-making state of affairs; it is simply inefficiency. Every successful teacher of music whom I know uses methodical approaches. The goals of musical experience and achievement are broad. Pupils are expected to reach these goals as listeners, performers and creators. But how can they listen rather than just hear? How can they perform or create without skills and literacy in music?

The creative writer can already manipulate language, the painter can already hold a paintbrush confidently and the dancer already has physical co-ordination; the musician starts with almost nothing. Clearly, the music teacher has a gigantic task. He must teach children how to listen, how to play instruments, how to read music, how to improvise and how to create with sensitive judgement. He can only do this through structured courses. All the established methodologies in music, whether for classes of children or for individual instruments, are structured. Singing, playing, score reading, even creative music-making, all can be organised into schemes which allow for musical growth and understanding. Whether a teacher devises his own courses or uses published methods is not important. A structured approach towards designing a syllabus is what matters most and I would regard it as being as important for a music teacher to pursue his work with progression in mind as it is for the teacher of any other subject.

Of the sample lessons, two accord with this principle without question. The recorder lesson could be one of many which contribute towards methodical recorder tuition. The theory lesson is one brick in the wall of musical theory. Each new concept forms the foundation for the next. The creative lesson is the doubtful activity in this context. To me, it looks very like a 'one-off' activity: great fun to participate in and fulfilling in many ways but not likely to contribute towards a sustained involvement in music as a school subject. All structured courses follow linear paths and the best of them progress slowly. (The Kodály Method and Orff-Schulwerk demonstrate this.) A structured course in creative music-making could do this also, but each new concept or skill must be limited so that the validity of the creative work is preserved within confines which are understood. In *Sound and Silence* by Paynter and Aston, many of the projects are useful *because of* the limitations imposed: restrictions of timbre, form or literary stimulus. A musical free-for-all is not based on strong educational foundations. The failure of the creative lesson demonstrates to me the importance of my third principle.

I have found the three guiding principles, outlined above, useful yardsticks for measuring the worth of classroom activities. They provide the lateral boundaries to the vertical concept of objectives. When an idea for a new activity arises, I simply ask these questions:

Is it suitable for everyone?
Is it an active pursuit?
Can I structure it?

If the answer to all three questions is 'yes', then I am satisfied that the activity will be of educational value. If the answer to any one question is 'no', I let the idea fade.

Most of the remaining chapters in this book deal with approaches which have been well tried in the classroom. All of them can accord with the three guiding principles. At the end of each chapter, two sample lessons are given.

This chapter has been much concerned with theoretical aspects of music teaching. The methods and activities described later in the book are essentially practical. I mentioned earlier how I felt that the philosophy of education lectures I attended as a student seemed to bear little relationship to the realities of the classroom. Similarly, the psychology lectures felt remote from the hurly-burly of school life. Before looking at various facets of music education, we will walk into a music classroom and see what it is like.

3 MATTERS OF FACT

Management and mismanagement

I was told of two ways of addressing a question to a class. One was to ask an individual for an answer while the other was to put a question to the whole class and to invite one of those who had their hands raised to answer. I thought this advice useful and my first question in my first lesson was directed to the whole class. We were singing 'Jamaica Farewell'. 'Where is Jamaica?' I asked. 'Hands up.' 'West Indies, Sir,' came a reply from somewhere at the back. I was immediately nonplussed by the options that flooded into my mind:

Should I admonish the disobedient child and make an example of him for calling out of turn?

Should I accept the answer and continue the lesson in the interests of pace and continuity?

Should I ignore the answer – i.e. pretend to be deaf – and put the same question to another child whose hand is dutifully waving in the air?

Should I censure the culprit and then ask another child if the answer is correct or not?

Should I wash my hands of the whole incident and continue the lesson as though I had never asked the question in the first place?

Unfortunately, I cannot remember what I did, but with experience I learned to vary my reaction to such events. I learned not to become too predictable. Analysing the incident and others like it, I realised that part of my task was to instil into the class a sense of professionalism. The child who called out was using his brain correctly, he was being enthusiastic, he was attending and he meant no ill-will. His only crimes were mild disobedience and unprofessionalism. Just as teachers generally behave as teachers should, so children generally behave as pupils should. For instance, teachers assume a responsibility for their pupils. Pupils recognise and respect that responsibility. Teachers set and mark homework. Pupils do homework. Teachers should turn up to their lessons on time. So should pupils. Teachers teach. Pupils learn. In almost every minute of school life, teachers and pupils have rôles to play. I suggest that, in a sense, the pupil's rôle is no less professional than the teacher's. Their professionalism might include the showing of initiative and lively responses. At other times it may demand more passivity. Most children are aware of what is expected of them and, in the great majority of schools, they do fulfil their rôle, their professionalism slotting in exactly with that of the teacher. Both are working towards the same ends and the 'we–they' view of school, if investigated, is not based on much substance. Where and when conflict arises, it often stems from teachers or pupils stepping outside this professional rôle. My reaction to unprofessional behaviour from pupils should, ideally, have the effect of assisting those pupils in becoming more professional. Once I had sorted this out in my mind, I felt no sense of shame in occasionally conducting a 'blitz' on student behaviour – that is, student professionalism. Of course, children do not always sit still, or listen to every word, or show consistently courteous behaviour, but they know that, for much of the time, they should. By showing our pupils that we expect them to act within the limits understood by most to be 'correct', we are helping them to behave as most of them would wish to. Evidence for this is found in the oft-heard remarks from children such as: 'Mrs Watkins is a good teacher: she keeps us under control.'

However, there are children who have no grasp of such professionalism and no wish to acquire it. Clearly, severely disruptive children must be referred to a higher authority within the school. The wildest children disturbed me considerably. I felt that I should be able to manage them and if, having tried, I found that I could not do so, I felt a sense of failure. Looking beyond the school, I observed that a significant proportion of adults has difficulty with the law. Commonsense tells us that antisocial tendencies are likely to manifest themselves before adulthood and it seems fair to congratulate schools and school teachers for containing junior troublemakers as well as they do without the benefit of courts and prisons. In other words, I grew to realise that misbehaviour was not entirely due to mismanagement on my part, but is a permanent feature of school life.

Despite the solace these thoughts brought me I remained worried about the effects of my tenuous control over some classes. It is well known that some teachers enjoy better discipline than others. As a probationary teacher, I was definitely one of the others. In my attempts to stamp some professionalism upon my classes, I resorted to punishments such as writing lines, detention and so on. But, each time I punished a child, I felt a qualm of conscience. Was I not punishing the child for my own ineptitude as a teacher? The answer was 'yes' in many cases and this provoked feelings of guilt. I think one *should* feel guilty about this and make every effort to adjust one's methods in order to avoid the cause of the guilt. There is some comfort to be had, however. Every craftsman must learn his craft. If our craft includes the handling of people, then it is likely that some of the people will suffer a little from our learning. We cannot obliterate the novice from life so we must live with him. If I have trouble with my classes, I must do something about it. But at the same time, I can stand outside myself a little and regard my classes as being unlucky for the time being. I will improve as a teacher and other classes will, in due course, benefit from my initial mistakes just as the classes who suffer from my inexperience now are no doubt benefiting from the mistakes made by their other, more mature, teachers when they were students.

Class control is a kind of performance and it is clear that effective performance best takes place in an orderly atmosphere. Once such an atmosphere has been established, everyday tips and aids can be put into effect. Advice of this sort is given in the books listed in the Appendix. Good voice projection, avoidance of mannerisms and catch phrases, clear blackboard work and the like are the bread and butter of good teaching, but I have found that they are not guarantees of success.

I could exercise reasonably firm control over my classes after a few terms of teaching but it was an effort. I returned home each day exhausted. I could not envisage myself lasting long as an active human being with such an erosion taking place. The cause of my fatigue became clear to me by chance. I was rehearsing a recorder group one lunch hour and noticed that two or three of the players were raising their fingers unnecessarily far from the instruments. 'Look at your own fingers', I suggested. 'How much of that movement is really playing the recorder? About a centimetre? Yet you are lifting your fingers three centimetres. Two thirds of your effort is not helping towards recorder playing.' Soon after this incident, an analogy presented itself to me:

> The recorder player should preserve his effort solely for playing the recorder. He should not dissipate it.
>
> The teacher should preserve his effort solely for teaching. He should not dissipate it.

What is teaching? For me, it was those moments of the day when I was consciously trying to effect a change in my pupils. These moments were quite infrequent, maybe two or three times a lesson. The rest of the lesson was spent in preparation for the teaching points, in practising skills, in consolidating known material. The teaching moments are the time for focus, the times when I exert my authority and gather the concentration of each individual on the matter to be taught. These moments demand the usual admonitions: 'Silence!', 'Look this way', 'Pay attention' etc. If the children are given a small ration of teaching points they are more likely to concentrate. They will sense that their attention is of professional importance. Conversely, if they are expected to learn continuously, they will become mentally exhausted. Similarly, I as the teacher, conserve my energies for the teaching points and remain comparatively relaxed in between. In this way, the exhaustion and the sense of burden are alleviated. Making a conscious effort to alter my style of teaching to this mode, I found that I worked less hard but taught more. I found that the children, having fewer demands made upon them, learned faster.

Singing lessons

I remember vividly the first music lesson I gave. It was a tug-of-war with myself. Sooner or later the children were going to have to make music. My thoughts went: 'Music = noise; noise = loss of control.' I was terrified that by inviting the children to play an active rôle in the lesson I would, at the same time, be inviting them to destroy the tiny element of authority which, as a student, I felt I might possess. The fear communicated itself to the class and was justified. Though I hardly provoked a riot, I witnessed respect and obedience diminish to almost nothing. The feeble singing which started the lesson caused me to plead: 'Sit up and sing up!' Suddenly the raucous, mocking tones of children licensed to give trouble dominated the room. 'Stop being so silly!', I said. 'When I asked you to sing up I didn't mean shout.' So the lesson went on, punctuated by threats and strictures, and fraught with tension. I was depressed by the experience. I felt I had taken on insurmountable problems. With help from the resident teacher, things got better rather than worse, but the main boost to my self-esteem came when I was asked to cover a geography lesson for an absent teacher. At first I was appalled when I was told that the class in question was one of the most ill disciplined in music lessons. The bell sounded. The children were lined up outside the geography room and I told them to go in. This they did, each person apparently having a set desk to occupy. They took out exercise books and textbooks, put their bags on the floor and settled down to the work written up on the blackboard. A few pupils lacked pens. I rummaged in the desk drawer, found some and handed them out, and prepared myself for forty minutes of duty as a prison warder. To my great astonishment, no such duty was needed. This class, which had filled me with fear and anxiety only yesterday, was getting on with its work. I gradually relaxed to the point of becoming bored. Eventually I picked up a geography textbook and read about map contours with some interest. The bell sounded again; there was a flurry of books into bags, a scraping of chair legs on the floor and a presentation of twenty-eight expectant faces waiting for the word of release. I took in the pens and let them go.

All this set me thinking. I realised that music is not like geography – in fact it is not like any other subject except, perhaps, physical education. It was not my weakness which caused the conflict between enthusiastic involvement and effective class management – the conflict lay in the subject itself. In an active music lesson, as in a physical education lesson, the children are being asked to let themselves go in a noisy or muscular way, yet at the same time they are expected to be sensitive to the boundaries of such freedom. It is so much more simple to ask children to think or to write or to do sums. They can think, write or calculate as hard as they like. It should offer no challenge to their teacher's authority.

Where could I find examples of such conflict being successfully resolved? I could watch other teachers but they were different. Their experience, age and sanction-backed authority rendered them inimitable by me, a student only a few years older than the children I was trying to teach. The answer never came on teaching practice. I became a professional musician instead and spent six years playing in orchestras under some fine conductors.

It was here that I found my answer. Music-making in class can be like a rehearsal. With those years of orchestral experience behind me, I found myself much better equipped to handle music lessons when I re-entered schools. In an orchestral rehearsal, each individual works towards the corporate effort and this entails an element of self-restraint. It was not the fear of losing one's job which brought about such self-discipline. It was simply a matter of professionalism and a clear vision of the value of the end product.

In a rehearsal, it is the detail of the music which is under scrutiny. Similarly, in a music lesson where there is corporate music-making, the detail should be the main focus of attention for everyone. Looking back at my student lesson, I blush to think how far from this concept my approach was. Admonitions such as 'Sing up!' and 'Not too loud!' were grossly inadequate – as inappropriate as they would be in a rehearsal of a professional choir or orchestra. Even with a simple song, I should have had a clear concept in my mind as to how the finished result should sound. If the spirit of the words and music is to be realised, then a methodical, businesslike approach to every aspect of the preparation and conduct of the lesson is called for.

The key questions are: 'What is wrong?' and 'How can I put it right?' Such questions may appear naive but it is astonishing how, at times, even professional conductors cannot ask them. A notable example is lodged in my memory. I was playing in one of the leading British orchestras and the conductor was rehearsing the 'New World Symphony' by Dvořák. 'We will just run through it', he said, and we did. After we had paused for breath he suggested that we have another look at the first few bars. We played through the whole symphony again. After the late coffee break, he said he was still uncertain about the opening of the symphony and this resulted in another uninterrupted run-through which completed the three-hour rehearsal. I could only conclude that he was unable to distinguish between what he heard and what he wanted to hear – that he was unable to ask (let alone answer) the questions: 'What is wrong?' and 'How can I put it right?'

In class there is nearly always room for improvement in musical terms. There is nearly always a difference between what we hear and what we want to hear. The diction of the words in a song, the proper use of the breath, the nuances of volume and expression: all are areas for close attention. In many ways a singing lesson is like a choir rehearsal and attention to detail is an essential requisite for gaining the involvement and disciplined co-operation of the children.

If the components of the music are the main objects of attention in a lesson, then the more components there are, the more purposeful the work will be, provided the result does not go beyond the capabilities of the children. So two-part songs, songs with instrumental accompaniment and songs with subtleties of rhythm and pitch will offer more scope for hard work than easy melodies sung in unison. I have noticed that when I introduce a simple adornment, such as a regular tambourine beat, to a song, the class will adopt immediately a more purposeful approach. As I ask the tambourine player to play his part on his own, the others in the class listen and watch with interest. When I rehearse one part of a two-part song with half the class, the other half will listen and express involvement through their very silence. When, in a strophic song, I give the verse to smaller groups of children in turn and use the full class to sing the chorus, the level of professionalism rises automatically.

The success of such an approach depends almost solely upon my ability to answer the two questions: 'What is wrong?' and 'How can I put it right?' In a singing lesson, some of the more common answers to the first question might be:

1 The rhythm in bar x is imprecise.
2 Some children cannot pitch correctly the interval in bar x.
3 The diction is poor in verse x.
4 The balance between the parts is unequal.
5 The singing is inexpressive in verse x.

Of course, many other problems can arise, but the ones listed above will serve as material for answering the second question: 'How can I put it right?'

1 Problem: Imprecise rhythm
   Solutions: Practice isolated passages slowly.
               Demonstrate on a percussion instrument.
               Use examples of the same rhythm from familiar songs.
2 Problem: Mispitching
   Solutions: Isolate the troublesome notes and turn them into a repetitive exercise.
               Transpose the passage up or down so that it lies more comfortably for the voice.
               Omit accompaniment, thus removing possibly distracting overtones.
               Use examples of the same interval from familiar songs.
3 Problem: Poor diction
   Solutions: Speak or whisper the words slowly and precisely.
               Examine where a vowel ends and a consonant begins.
               Practise the passage with exaggerated diction and then 'tone down' to an acceptable level.
4 Problem: Unequal balance
   Solutions: Locate the cause of weakness in the quieter part (problems 1, 2 or 3) and put it right.
               Move a strong singer from one part to the other.
               Record the class and play back in order to clarify the weakness to the performers.
5 Problem: Inexpressive singing
   Solutions: Introduce a wider dynamic range.
               Attend to expression marks in the music or introduce some if they are absent.
               Discuss the meaning of the words.

The need for analytical precision in rehearsal is paramount. Though there is a place for straight repetition in order to familiarise the class with the music, most of the activity must have a purpose and the purpose should be explained clearly. The purpose of rehearsal is to narrow the gap between what we hear and what we wish to hear. It is to put right those features of the music-making which we hear to be faulty.

Instrumental lessons

Lessons with instruments should be conducted in a similar manner to the vocal lessons, but there are further factors for consideration and these are dealt with below. The choice and acquisition of instruments will be discussed at the end of the chapter.

Generally speaking, children do not 'tootle' with their voices, but they are inclined to do so with instruments. The temptation to have a random shot at a glockenspiel bar or to have just a *tiny* puff down a recorder is almost irresistible. Until a student teacher feels fairly certain that his authority has been established sufficiently to control this kind of behaviour, he is advised to treat instrumental work with extra caution. The advice below is of a general nature, since detailed investigation into various kinds of instrumental work appears in other chapters. Similarly, creative work and the teaching techniques associated with it appear elsewhere also.

Whether the lesson be for recorders alone or for the full panoply of instrumental hardware, orderly distribution is important since it sets the tone for the whole lesson. Some teachers set out the instruments on tables before the class arrives. This is not always possible so let us assume that the instruments are stored in a cupboard. Remember that this is a rehearsal as well as a lesson, and the establishment of proper rehearsal procedures is part of the children's musical education. This being so, no apology is needed for teaching the children *not* to play. I emphasise this point because I have experienced, and have seen students experience the monstrous crescendo of undisciplined cacophony which started from one child 'just testing' an F sharp on a glockenspiel. While the instruments are being distributed, random playing is an offence. The teacher is well advised to keep the children out of temptation's path. If he does not do so, the offence is partly his. He can effect this by telling the children to keep the recorders in their boxes or covers until told to unpack them; he can distribute the beaters for the tuned percussion after the instruments have been given out; and the general instruction to leave the instruments on the tables or desks helps also to create a good working atmosphere from the start. For the very first lesson and for perhaps a few of the following ones, it is best to stand by the cupboard and hand out instruments to each child individually as they file past. The next stage is to appoint specific children to distribute the instruments to the class and, incidentally, to collect them in again at the end of the lesson. When the children are used to instrumental work and when they are properly trained in the manners of a rehearsal, they can collect their instruments in a less regimented way. If this advice seems cautious and authoritarian it is because experience has shown how an excess of freedom can lead to serious disorder.

With mixed instrumental work, organise the seating so that sections are grouped together in a sensible manner. If necessary, clear to the side unwanted furniture to make room for music stands. Glockenspiel and xylophone players often prefer to stand when playing, so place them at the back of the classroom.

The children will play when they are told to, but if they are not asked to play at all for twenty minutes, as can happen if detailed work with one section of the class gets bogged down, restlessness is inevitable. The balance of an instrumental rehearsal is crucial to its success. In a vocal lesson the technical details are not always obvious. In an instrumental lesson, they can sometimes be too obvious, with a corresponding excess of time spent upon some detail. This applies to mixed instrumental work in particular. With single-timbre ensembles like recorder, percussion band or harmonica, the problem is less severe.

In order to reach all the players in a short space of time, two guides to rehearsal technique are useful. The first is to practise only fragments of the music with any one section of the class at any one time – say four bars rather than eight. Having rehearsed each section in this way, put it all together. Using this method, each player will have played at least twice. Then go on to the next four bars and so on. The other guide is to pace out expectations of excellence. Some children can be infuriatingly slow to grasp what, to us, seem the simplest of skills and concepts. We can fall into the trap of expecting dramatic improvements to take place under our eyes. When this fails to happen, we are tempted to beaver away at one problem with one group of children in order to fulfil our expectations of excellence. But, of course, the other children are losing interest. It is more important to reach everyone quickly, working for small, sometimes barely perceptible improvements, than it is to make large laborious advances with a few children. Many small improvements lead eventually to a large one and, in this way, activity for all is maintained.

Some general points concerning rehearsal management should be considered. The music room is well equipped with objects to hide behind, psychologically if not physically. Among them are the piano, the conductor's stand, the desk, the table with audio equipment on it, and maybe, a pair of timps strategically placed between you and 'them'. The plunge into making real music should be matched by a physical plunge. If you move around between the pupils, if you use your singing voice as well as the piano to demonstrate points, if you show as well as instruct, you will involve your class and be involved with them more fruitfully.

Learn the techniques of the instruments with which you are dealing. The most simple expedients will improve the sound wonderfully. Many children dampen the notes they are playing on tuned percussion by allowing the beater to rest on the bar. A bouncing action will bring forth a much better tone. Tambourines sound more characteristic if gravity is allowed to work on the jingles. All stringed instruments give more pleasure when they are properly tuned. And so it might go on: do not play the piano too loudly, choose music of an appropriate standard, keep instruments disinfected and in good repair. What it all boils down to is commonsense and good musical judgement. Nearly all music teachers can sing and/or play an instrument. Attendance at rehearsals of choirs and orchestras as participants can teach us a great deal about rehearsal techniques. These skills can and should be used in the classroom.

Listening lessons

There are plenty of activities in music lessons where rehearsal techniques are not appropriate. One such is the lesson which involves audio equipment. However many warnings we may receive, sooner or later, we all play the wrong track on a record, run the record player at the wrong speed, put an empty cassette into the deck or record a class performance without pressing the record button. These incidents are entertaining every now and again, but damaging if they occur too often. I have found that the easiest and safest approach is to ensure that all the recorded material needed for a lesson is on cassette tape with beginning and ending numbers of extracts carefully noted. The advantages are too obvious to list. However, the underlying intention has implications for the conduct of a lesson which contains an element of listening.

If the material for listening is to be well prepared, then the music to be listened to must also be deserving of close attention. I have often heard student teachers shout above the music: 'That's an oboe. It's meant to sound like a cock crowing and that means it's morning', thus dissipating any atmosphere created by the sensitive ending of *Danse Macabre*. This pinpoints the problems inherent in a 'listening' lesson. There is no way of knowing whether individuals are listening to or gaining anything from the music. The fear of the children talking, nudging each other, passing notes or indicating their lack of interest by any other means can cause a teacher to pre-empt such behaviour by providing a running commentary, sometimes punctuated by reprimands and threats. It seems to me that the moments when music rules the atmosphere of the class rather than the class ruling the atmosphere of the music are few indeed. For this reason, I feel that recorded music is best used as a tool for musical achievement through objectives related to literacy skills and specific knowledge rather than to aesthetic benefits unsupported by other aspects of music education. An example of the former is score-reading exercises which serve to build up literacy skills alongside awareness of timbre, form and so on. Another is the use of recorded music to focus attention upon the achievements of the class in their creative and re-creative work. A little differently, re-creative work can give more scope to listening. A Spanish song has obvious connections with Spanish music; performance of a minuet on classroom instruments can lead to an understanding of minuet form and lead towards intelligent listening to a minuet. Similarly, links between playing and listening to music in pop and rock idioms are clearly to be taken advantage of.

Classroom instruments, audio equipment and books

Recorders

Most teachers use descant instruments to the exclusion of other sizes. Trebles present a problem of different fingering while tenors can be too large for younger children to manage. Still, the presence of treble and tenor recorders is advantageous though they do bring extra teaching problems with them.

Plastic recorders with three joints offer the widest scope. They can be tuned, they are easy to clean and on some models the bottom joint will turn to allow for players who prefer to use their left hand for the lower notes. If a child insists on playing the recorder the wrong way round, it seems better to accommodate his quirk than to upset, destroy possibly, the skill he has acquired so far. Recorders should be disinfected between lessons and trays designed for this purpose are available.

Glockenspiels

A mixture of soprano and alto glockenspiels is useful but it must be remembered that the alto models occupy more space on a table and in a storage cupboard. Chromatic models offer much more scope than diatonic, even when the latter are supplied with optional F sharps and B flats. The soprano sounds an octave higher than the written notes. The alto plays at pitch. Most makes of glockenspiel have rubber buffers between the bars and the body of the instrument. This rubber can be picked off quite easily by irresponsible fingers. Spare rubber, which comes in the form of a tube for some models, is available. The beaters supplied with some educational glockenspiels can be inadequate in that they are too light in weight, easily broken or precariously constructed, the rubber ball-like head flying off the wooden handle with irritating frequency. It is quite simple to make beaters and equally simple, though more expensive, to buy spares. I have noticed a kind of inertia creep over some music teachers in this corner of music education. I have seen a neat row of pupils tapping the instruments with pencil ends, combs and front door keys. The musical results were not impressive.

Xylophones

These are expensive but as they add a pleasing solidity to the jangling of glockenspiels, they are well worth acquiring. Orff-Schulwerk has brought these instruments into the limelight and a variety of models is seen in catalogues. Soprano, alto and bass instruments form the basis of the family. The bass instrument is expensive: the cost of one chromatic bass xylophone is roughly equivalent to that of one hundred and fifty descant recorders. Beaters can cost extra. Always think of storage before you buy.

Metallophones

A sort of cross between a glockenspiel and a xylophone, the metallophone consists of metal bars placed across a resonating chamber. They vary and enrich the classroom sound and are available in soprano, alto and bass sizes. They are generally cheaper than xylophones.

Untuned percussion

Here, personal choice must be the guide. A few of the lesser-known instruments should be mentioned however. A tambour is like a tambourine without jingles and is useful for keeping a basic beat going. The guiro looks like a fish with a serious skin ailment. The ridged surface makes an exciting snarl when scraped with a stick of hardwood. The Cabassa consists of a solid cylinder of wood (like an extra-large, old-fashioned cotton reel) attached to a handle. Around the cylinder are linked metal balls which grate against the rough metal lining. The sound is similar to that of maracas but louder and easier to control. Claves consist of a pair of rods, one of which is struck against the other. Often they can be used with success by less able children. Beware of the fibreglass models which can leave microscopic splinters of glass on the hands.

Harmonicas

These are useful classroom instruments in that they play in tune, can play chords, blend well with other instruments and are easy to handle in the earlier stages. However, disinfection is a little awkward as the reeds can be damaged easily. Diatonic instruments in C are recommended. Chromatic instruments are a lot more expensive, and the lever is liable to bend rendering the instrument useless.

Melodicas

A miniature organ blown by the player. Melodicas come in various sizes and shapes. The blowing tube should be regarded as *de rigueur* for both ease of playing and hygiene.

Guitars

A few guitars help the classroom ensemble substantially, but beware of the cheapest which are difficult to tune and come with wire strings. Ways of using guitars with unskilled children are discussed in chapter 5.

Electric guitars

The electric bass guitar is becoming recognised as an exceptionally useful classroom instrument. So often, the 'educational' sound lacks bass. This instrument helps to remedy that lack. It is best entrusted to a child who already has some skill on a stringed instrument. Instant results should not be expected. Exercise great caution when buying second-hand electrical equipment.

Chordal instruments

The chord organ has a short keyboard for the right hand and rows of buttons for the left hand. The buttons play either single bass notes or major or minor chords. The major chords cover most of the requirements of classroom music but the minor chords generally do not. For instance, B flat minor is available but E minor is absent from some models. Often, the keys are narrower than those on a piano and this can cause an experienced pianist to play wrong notes. Some types of electric keyboard (a computerised version of the chord organ) have similar limitations with regard to size, but they do offer a full range of chords.

The Autoharp and Chromaharp are instruments which play zither-like chords. The notes are automatically selected through the depression of bars. They add substance to the classroom sound but are limited in tonal range and need elaborate tuning.

The piano-harp

This is a piano (generally upright), stripped of its keyboard, its action and its front panels, revealing a criss-cross of strings which can offer all sorts of musical opportunities, especially for non-notated creative work. It is difficult to know which pitch belongs to which string (though they can be labelled). However, the strings can be struck with glockenspiel beaters, stroked with a ruler, plucked with finger-nails and played in a variety of other ways. Try to rescue a piano on its journey to the municipal dump and convert it to a piano-harp for classroom use.

Audio equipment

In this area the choice is enormous. Local education authorities are inclined still to provide schools with elderly wooden cases containing sturdy, sensible hardware. If you are given some choice in the matter, buy non-portable equipment, so that other departments in the school are not given the chance to damage it through misuse. The requirements of the dance teacher who has to lug the record player from gym to hall to drama studio are very different from those of the music teacher. Make sure that you are supplied with equipment which will record from record deck to cassette deck with ease. Good live recording facilities are essential. The 'recording session' is often the high point of a creative or re-creative lesson and only good quality equipment will do justice to the children's work.

Some teachers make use of portable cassette tape recorders and/or synthesisers, especially with C.S.E. groups. Others construct 'teaching programmes' on tapes which children listen to through ear pieces or headphones. This allows individuals to work at their own pace.

Exercise books, sheet music and files

I have noticed that exercise books seldom suit the requirements of the music teacher. Often, only half a dozen pages are used in a year. The book whose pages are half manuscript and half lined for writing is little better. The two halves get out of phase with the result that pages are wasted. If musical literacy is important to you, then use pure manuscript books. If you do not expect to use books very much, do not use them at all, but employ single sheets of lined or manuscript paper when they are needed. A cheap source of manuscript paper can be obtained by running a blank manuscript 'master' through a spirit copier. The various pieces of paper can be put into files of the most basic construction – pieces of stiff card folded once with holes punched for treasury tags. When the course is finished, the files can be used again, either with other classes or else for sheet music.

Sheet music can become a source of serious headaches. At the close of an orchestral rehearsal you might be left to pick it off the floor and from behind radiators. 'Eve Level' gets mixed up with the *Radetzky March* and, at the end of a long day, the pile of tattered papers seems to speak of ungrateful pupils and despair. If the children are told to look after their own, the music can get lost or become even more ragged. If one of the first oboe players is ill, the other has no copy to play from at the next rehearsal.

A simple solution is to keep the music in files, the same as those used in class for occasional work. The sheet music should be punched with holes and tagged into the files, each file being labelled on the outside: 'First Violin, Desk 1' and so on. As a programme builds up, so the music in the file builds up. After the concert the parts can be removed, sorted and stacked in the usual way. If you run several groups, say an orchestra, a string orchestra, a wind band and a recorder consort, each group should have its own set of files of unique colour.

The piano

I have left discussion of the piano till the end of the chapter because it plays a part in so many kinds of lesson. We must assume that you are supplied with a piano and that, whatever its quality, you have to live with it. The horizontal (grand) piano has advantages in the classroom in that you can see over it. This gives you flexibility in where you position it. The upright acts often as a screen between you and your class. In this case, the obvious remedy is to move the piano into a position where you can read the music and see the children at the same time, albeit at an oblique angle. This may entail re-arranging all the furniture but the fifteen minutes spent on the manoeuvre will be well used.

The main reason for having the whole class in view is to be able to make contact and to carry out the work efficiently and pleasantly. The necessity for spotting trouble is secondary. Trouble can start under your nose and, conversely, it may fail to arise when you are out of the classroom for ten minutes. An indication to the children that they might be under surveillance (surely an invitation to misbehave) in a music lesson is the sight of the teacher standing while playing the piano. Some teachers manage to play adequately this way and rouse no antagonism in their classes. However, I have found it more effective to play sitting down. The natural position helps to promote a relaxed and purposeful lesson.

In the chapters which follow, some of the main methodologies and trends in music education are described – described, but not dissected. In most cases, there is an abundance of literature which puts forward the arguments and explains the pedagogy. References to this literature are made in the text. However, some practices, though widely known, have received little attention in books and journals. In these cases, I have offered a fuller description.

Curiously, few British teachers of music put all their skill and commitment into one method or philosophy. There is a tendency to borrow from here and there, to adapt materials and to maintain flexible independence. Taking this reality as my starting point, I shall present a picture of some of the existing practices in music education and suggest ways in which one might involve the ideas and materials in a broadly based scheme of work.

4 VOCAL MUSIC IN THE CLASSROOM

As a student, I read a number of books on the teaching of music. All of them offered ample advice on the teaching of singing. More recently, I have read books and articles which have suggested other, more divergent, ways of using the voice. Nowhere have I encountered an opinion which has placed realistic emphasis upon two of the most important facts of life in the music classroom. The first is that there is always a number of children who cannot sing; the second is that there is always a number of children who will not sing. The first group ('growlers', 'droners', 'monotones') are mentioned in the books as are the changing voices of boys which traditionally form the second group. According to some of the authors I read, I could override problems like these through skilful and purposeful teaching. I will admit here that I could not. Not always, that is. Though I learned to accommodate monotones either by giving them an instrument to play, by giving them some remedial lessons in break times or by simply tolerating their toneless and tuneless contributions, I could not induce a class to sing if it did not want to.

It may seem illogical to refer to a 'class' as wanting something or not when it consists of thirty individuals, each with his or her own free will, but it certainly was the 'class' which would not sing. A few members might try to co-operate in a depressingly noncommittal manner, but they narrowed their dynamic range to a consistent *mezzoforte* and slurred their diction as a matter of course. I could not blame them. Like them, I would not want to stand out as an enthusiast in a pool of apathy. Like them, I would resign myself to being a member of a 'class that would not sing'. Classes of this sort emerged in mysterious ways. There were none in the first year (eleven-year-olds), a few in the second and many in the third. While an occasional third-year class sang lustily and skilfully, most would remain resolutely uncooperative. It made me wonder at times whether 'the child', so often referred to by educational theorists, really existed. Each of my classes contained 'the child', yet the behaviour I encountered was so varied. Surely 'the child' either does sing when he reaches the age of thirteen or he does not. Maybe the answer is that 'the child' *sometimes* sings when he reaches the age of thirteen.

I have dwelt on this point because I feel strongly that singing is useful in music lessons only when the children will sing. If they will not, then it seems more sensible to abandon singing as an activity for the promotion of musical experience and achievement. Obviously, the children will not experience or achieve anything. However, we must be careful to distinguish between a refusal to sing and a reluctance to *start* singing. If we can overcome the children's and our inhibition, we might break through a barrier which turns out to be less formidable than at first it appears.

Singing is a social activity. The ability to 'let go', to accept abnormal utterance as normal, is an essential prerequisite. In drama lessons, pupils are expected to make pretend and to unbottle their feelings. In movement lessons, they unstiffen and explore the pleasures of mobility in ways which would appear most peculiar if enacted in the supermarket. Similarly, singing is a specialised activity which can offer satisfaction and pleasure to nearly everyone, provided the time is right (which it is in a music lesson) and provided the pupils are introduced to their own singing voices in a convincing manner.

Although there is plenty of guidance in books on how to pursue a course of classroom or choral singing, there is almost none on how to nurture the first notes. In a recorder lesson, we can instruct the class to place their fingers and thumbs just so and then blow. What is the equivalent in vocal education? The following extract from a B.B.C. broadcast given by Esther Salaman in 1978 offers advice on how to set up favourable conditions for class singing:

> There are three basic needs which, when worked together, allow the voice to emerge freely, without strain. One: a 'tall' stance encouraging support of the breath with a kind of 'squeeze' in and up from low down, the groin, in fact. Two: the resilient ever-open throat (where we swallow and yawn, at the pharynx). And three: closely in league with this, openness at the back of the throat − the ever-alert, bright countenance with all the little muscles working around nose, cheeks, eyes and higher still, awakening the higher resonance and influencing the position of the soft palate.
>
> This 'trinity' of muscular gestures aligned together feels like an athletic sense of unity. From this one can work straight away into the feel of 'centering' the tone of every vowel to its very heart, bringing vitality, vibrance, and the individual quality of each voice. Resonance can find its own way around, 'lighting up' every alerted cranny of our instruments, giving colour, harmonic richness and balanced intonation.
>
> When children accept the comfortable feelings of these basic skills (without having to understand the technical language I have just used) the fun begins, for them and for the teacher. True, when children begin to grow very tall very fast, around twelve and over, their 'lower halves' nearly lose their 'upper halves' as they try to support their breath. But most of the time, the feeling of a well harnessed overall strength is sufficient to meet all vocal situations without strain.

One may question whether every pupil will be prepared to co-operate in this way. However, if they observe that *our* attitude is professional, that we are not simply treating singing as a kind of speech with notes added, they may well feel inclined to join in.

Another approach which has been used with success is to work towards singing through the use of classroom instruments. An example might be as follows. Copies of a song and its chord symbols are handed to the children. They are instructed to prepare versions of the song using voices and instruments in ways they think suitable, working in groups of five or six. As the activity develops (and it may take more than one lesson) the children are inclined to sing almost despite themselves, until the inhibition which characterised the early stages of the work disappears. After listening to one another's arrangements, the class can sing the song together. At this stage, attention can be drawn to basic matters of posture and voice production.

Children are more likely to respond well in the upper forms if they have enjoyed worthwhile vocal activities in the lower forms and at primary school. So it is the earlier experiences which are referred to in this chapter. Though the implication that the class *will* respond is ever present, I acknowledge that, of all musical activities, singing can be the most difficult to propagate with full success.

Though I enjoyed singing myself, I have often wondered what its purpose is in music education. I began to realise that the benefits of singing are diffuse and not necessarily connected with one another. I have organised them below under five headings.

1 *Vocal technique:* the mere act of singing skilfully is a rewarding experience.
2 *Musical literacy:* through singing children can learn notation.
3 *Repertoire:* with no special equipment the children can become familiar with the national heritage of folk song, the best of easy art song and popular song.
4 *Recreation:* the social benefits of singing can be enjoyed on the school outing coach, at the football stadium or in the pub in later life. Singing is fun.
5 *Vocal creativity:* imaginative use of the voice can produce expressive and impressive musical artifacts.

In most singing lessons that I have taken myself or seen others take, one or more of these categories has been central to the objective. However, a sixth category has intruded itself into my list:

6 *Stop-gap:* singing is an easy way of filling up a music lesson.

There does appear to be a large number of music teachers who feel that singing and forty minutes are fated to walk hand in hand and that it is nobody's business to interfere with such a happy marriage. I have come to realise that a commitment to singing in the classroom does not *in itself* provide an especially strong basis for classroom practice. I now feel that any commitment should be made toward one or more of the benefits listed above. It is from this viewpoint that vocal activities are discussed in the remainder of this chapter.

Vocal technique

Singing is a skill and like other skills it requires a structured approach. The areas for development include the correct use of the various 'voices' (head, chest etc.), the proper methods of breathing in and out, the control of tone and volume, the niceties of diction, intonation, the holding of an independent part, varied articulation and projection. If one were to concentrate on all these aspects of vocal technique in every class singing lesson, the class would soon become a choir. The question of structuring these skills concurrently is intriguing indeed.

Two methods of structured vocal education are well tried. Curwen's Tonic Sol-fa Method was enormously successful in the late nineteenth century and is enjoying a revival today. Kodály's Method is based firmly on Curwen's in many respects and has gained wide support outside its native Hungary. It is Kodály's Method which will receive attention here because it is well established and well structured and covers a number of the headings under consideration, notably vocal technique, literacy and repertoire. Details of the Method can be obtained from *Kodály's Principles in Practice* by Szönyi and *The Kodály Way to Music* by Vajda. Szönyi's book shows how well the Method suits a schooling system where the curriculum is standardised throughout the country and where rival attractions like classroom instruments and ideas of creative music-making offer less competition. Vajda's book, on the other hand, shows what can be done through appropriate adaptation for use in Britain. What is needed further is adaptation for older children. Vajda assumes that the Method will be applied at first to infant children. Such a luxury is rare, so ways must be found for introducing it at junior and secondary levels.

The aspects of the Kodály Method which concern vocal technique are relevant to any age group. Early on in the Method, Kodály introduces part singing. This serves two purposes. Firstly, it teaches independence which in itself builds up a sense of confidence and the listening faculty. Secondly, it heightens awareness of intonation problems and their solution. Kodály insisted that class singing should be unaccompanied: 'The tempered, or rather mistempered tonal degrees of the piano are unsuitable for aiding accurate and correct choral singing; it should neither be used for setting the pitch nor for accompaniment' (Szönyi, p. 13). The first experiences of two-part singing are introduced through exercises, not songs, and it seems that these work well with any age group. It is in the latter stages that divergence from the Method is called for. Publications like *Something to Sing, Book 3* by Geoffrey Brace offer attractive two-part material with piano accompaniment. There seems to be no good reason for spurning it for the sake of a principle which was formulated for different educational and cultural conditions. Kodály's Method is based on musical literature. That is, the technical teaching points grow out of the songs which are taught first. Points of singing technique should derive from the music also. A judicious choice of songs will demand progressively greater breath control and progressively wider dynamic and expressive ranges as the course proceeds.

It is not my purpose to offer instruction in the techniques of singing here. This aspect of music education is covered in other books. It is the structuring of the work that seems important. Though technical points should arise naturally from the songs, the songs themselves should be chosen with the development of technique in mind. For instance, if an increase in the vocal range is the objective, then songs will be taught in an order that facilitates a gradual extension of the range both upwards and downwards. If improved breath control is the objective, then special attention should be paid to phrase lengths and their demands. Where part-singing is the focus of attention, simple two-part songs will precede the complex ones. A problem arises when combinations of these and other aspects of vocal technique are to be taught simultaneously. Clearly, a totally logical structuring of vocal technique is impossible, but on the other hand, random choices of material are bound to inhibit progress. I think the best approach is to select a wide range of attractive and useful songs and almost literally to lay them on the floor like pieces of a jigsaw puzzle. They can be arranged into an order which best supports the teaching of all aspects of vocal technique. The result is a virtual textbook of class singing. In suggesting this, I am fully aware that songs come from different sources. The final 'textbook' will, in reality, be merely a list of songs. In working through the list, we might use half a dozen different songbooks, manuscript copies or B.B.C. pamphlets. However many books or pieces of paper there are, the over-riding importance of structure should give new impetus to the singing lesson.

Literacy

Kodály's teaching of pitch is based firmly on sol-fa in the early stages. Starting with the playground chant of a falling minor third (soh-mi), the children build up a stock of intervallic clichés, each one featured in suitable songs. In time, the pentatonic scale is established and this eventually leads to major and minor scales. This progression is similar to Curwen's as is Kodály's use of hand signs. The teacher gestures in the air using hand positions which have permanent associa-tions with sol-fa notation. A skilful teacher conducts two-part singing by using the hands independently. Kodály employs the rhythmic symbols of standard notation as opposed to the dots and dashes of the Curwen Method to indicate note lengths. However, before written notation is introduced, Kodály advocates the use of the French time names. The transfer from sol-fa to staff notation is rather complex and can be a cause of some confusion in the minds of children. It is here that other approaches seem sensible. Whereas in Hungary most school music is vocal, in Britain instrumental work occupies a prominent position and the use of staff notation is assumed for such work. I see no reason why children should not learn both staff notation and sol-fa concurrently. Eventually, sol-fa will be dropped from the singing lesson and staff notation, already familiar to the children through their instrumental work, will gently take its place. Children can learn French and German at the same time without serious confusion. If 'song' can be *chanson* and *Lied*, cannot the note 'G' be 'doh' (or any other sol-fa pitch name) and

Having observed the Kodály Method in action, I am convinced that it teaches musical literacy through sol-fa with success. If one's aim is to teach literacy

through singing, the Kodály Method is as good as any, provided one equates sol-fa with musical literacy.

Unfortunately, sol-fa is not the common language of musicians and many of us are unwilling to make ourselves sufficiently familiar with it in order to teach through it. There is no consistency in published material. Some B.B.C. pamphlets try to cover staff notation and sol-fa simultaneously, while certain songbooks (*Appuskidu*, *Ta-ra-ra Boom-de-ay* etc.) omit notation altogether from the pupil's books. The most common practice in songbook publication is for the words to be printed beneath staff notation. Pupils using these books are inclined to read the words, ignore the notes and pick up the melody by ear. My own experience suggests to me that only sol-fa can teach precision of pitch to unskilled children. Staff notation is useful for the teaching of rhythm, however, and the notes provide a useful guide to shapes of phrases as well. With the more committed pupils, this can lead to a level of precision in reading music which compares favourably with sol-fa trained voices. In *The Kodály Way to Music*, Vajda chooses songs with great skill, so that new concepts of rhythm *and* pitch are introduced in a sequence which is logical to both. Alas, most of the songs are not suited to older pupils (e.g. 'Lulla, Lulla, Sleep My Teddy, Lulla'), so an entirely new selection must be made even though the theoretical points contained therein might be the same. Assuming that staff notation is used, I suggest that rhythmic logic should be the governing factor and that details of pitch education be given a subsidiary rôle. There are plenty of songs with straightforward rhythms. These can serve to build up simple musical literacy which can be reinforced through instrumental work and score reading. In order to do this, the notes of the song should be studied by the children without the words. At first, the rhythms can be clapped, then the song sung to lah. Slow patient practice can lead to genuine sight-singing and simple literacy.

Repertoire

If we take the three areas mentioned under this heading on page 31, namely folk song, art song and popular song, structural teaching methods seem hardly appropriate. We must decide which branches of the vocal repertoire are important and work accordingly. Kodály insisted that 'Hungarian folk music is to become the child's musical mother-tongue' (Szönyi, p. 13). Should a British teacher be equally dogmatic about British folk music? In order to answer this question it would be wise to investigate briefly the 'cultural' issue in music education.

A case for the avant-garde, for pop, for rock, for medieval or for folk can be made with eloquence and, at times, with a zeal bordering on bigotry. Such cases are based on false assumptions: that the young only like pop music or that the avant-garde is the only genuine music of today. I must admit to some confusion here in that I enjoy all sorts of songs and my criteria for including any one song in my teaching programme rest on matters far removed from cultural preference. I find John Paynter's 'Autumn' very appealing. I also enjoy 'Yesterday' by Paul

McCartney. If I were forced into a 'cultural music policy', one of these songs would have to go. My choice would be based normally on the educational potential of a song rather than on its cultural associations. The development of breath control and true intonation is offered in 'Autumn' while points of musical theory (among other things) can be extracted from 'Yesterday'. It seems better to offer children the widest possible range of songs rather than, like Kodály, to restrict them to one musical culture. Songs are music and their study should be musical. Notions of heritage or idiomatic superiority are surely exclusive and outdated.

Singing for recreation

Singing for recreation does not mean solely singing for enjoyment. One hopes that every sort of singing will be enjoyed in any case. No doubt teachers of all subjects prefer their classes to enjoy their work. For many of us, deeper enjoyment derives from involvement and learning. It is often absent from the more passive pursuits like watching television. On the surface, recreation might appear to be merely a description of those moments in our lives which are not occupied by working, sleeping and eating: the parties, clubs, hobbies, chats over the fences which punctuate our existence. Yet often, these moments of recreation demand 'correct' behaviour as much as any other. If we cannot dance we feel gauche at a party; if we fail to keep abreast of current affairs we cannot contribute intelligently to certain conversations; and in the pub, if we are ignorant of well-known songs, we intone nonsense syllables on New Year's Eve and hope nobody notices.

Knowledge of popular song is a social necessity at times. An awareness of this can lead us to feel that it is our duty as music teachers to supply each generation of pupils with its ration of 'Ilkley Moors' and 'Clementines'. Knowledge of notation is unnecessary; 'correct' singing is not an issue – indeed, refinement could be a disadvantage; national culture is only remotely connected in that the songs in common use derive from all nations and levels of culture. The importance of this branch of music education should not be underestimated. The proliferation of Community Songbooks in the 1920s and 1930s was a symptom of the need felt at that time for a renewal of the community feeling aroused through singing. It is most unlikely that the national daily papers will sponsor such a movement now as they did then, so it is encumbent upon music teachers to keep the social skill alive. Whereas vocal skill and musical literacy are fairly fixed concepts in the minds of music teachers from one generation to the next, social music-making changes constantly. It is not so much that songs are ruthlessly dropped from the repertoire as that new ones are always being added. Most of them come from the popular sphere: from musical shows and from the commercial pop scene. They seem to require a little hallowing by time before they can enter the realm of recreational singing. Children on coaches seem to prefer singing 'oldies' by the Beatles or numbers from 'Joseph' to current hits. Knowledge of these songs must derive from listening to their parents' old records! Perhaps it should derive more from their music lessons – lessons which may appear to a casual listener wandering past the classroom door like the scorned time-filler, but which are actually serving an important social function.

Vocal creativity

Creative music-making is discussed in some detail in chapter 6. My concern here is with certain aspects of *vocal* creativity. At once, it would be best to drop the word creative as an all-embracing heading for this activity. It is the less traditional aspects of vocal work which are under discussion. Very often, they are strongly teacher directed and hardly creative at all. Suggestions for divergent vocal activities can be found in the writings of George Self, John Paynter and Murray Schafer. *When Words Sing* by Schafer is the most comprehensive if at times the least conventional.

Most of us harbour rather fixed notions about what our voices should be doing in given situations. We would be embarrassed to sing an after-dinner speech. Conversely, we can sense the discomfort of our tone-deaf neighbour at the carol service who is mumbling 'O Come all ye Faithful' on a monotone. We are inclined to make our voices, like our behaviour, conform to the expectations of society. Screaming, crying, laughter and other human noises are appropriate in certain circumstances but not in all.

It seems that advocates of divergent vocal work are asking us to reconsider our assumptions about the uses of the voice. The music of Ligeti, Berio and Stockhausen offers examples of artistic transformations of vocal 'noises'. Elements of chance, the use of electronic distortion and a general broadening of the concept of what music is present teachers with new and sometimes frightening areas for investigation and teaching. Two examples of unconventional vocal work in class might serve to illustrate the possibilities.

Every child in the class is asked to 'imagine' a note, perhaps a very high or low one. As the teacher points to each child in turn, so he hums his note quietly, resisting every temptation to consciously blend with the sounds around him. Eventually, a huge eerie chord suggestive of space and the unknown is built up. Through gesture, the teacher may produce cresendos or reduce the chord to near silence. The children breath randomly, so, in a class of thirty, the general effect may be continued for some time.

Each pupil is given a newspaper cutting. He must read it through slowly and silently. Each participant has his own word. It might be 'the' or 'and'. Every time he encounters 'his' word, he speaks it out loud. He may be asked to utter it as a high-pitched staccato bark or to adopt a languid drawl. With everyone participating in this game of controlled chance, the result is a pointillist soundscape of intriguing verbal textures and silences.

Two questions about this activity present themselves. What are we teaching the children? In what way can the results assume validity?

In an earlier chapter I suggested that educational processes bring about discernible changes. A brief review of the various types of vocal education demonstrates this. If we are concerned with vocal technique, we will expect a class to be able to sing more accurately or with a better sound than before. If we are teaching musical literacy through singing, the children's ability to read music will have improved. In the realm of repertoire, we are increasing the children's knowledge of worthwhile songs. Similarly, we might be increasing the children's ability to socialise musically. In each case, the change should be discernible, measurable even.

In the lessons described above, it might seem that the teacher is using the class as an agent in a trick. The results are unusual, exciting at times, and produced by the simplest of means, but it could be argued that, despite this, the children learn nothing, develop no skill and are being led blindly from nowhere to nowhere via nowhere. Even their listening skills are not being developed, for in order to play their part in either activity, they must work hard to ignore the contributions of others. The activity requires almost no skill, no literacy, no cultural awareness and very little sensitivity. So what is being taught?

The answer must depend on the answer to the second question: in what way can the results assume validity? If the sounds produced can be regarded as 'music', then, in producing them, the children must be partaking of a musical experience. We are so imbued with tonal music and functional harmony, we cannot contemplate easily the notion that Mozart or Mahler might not be 'valid'. For most of us, the mainstream of Western music is the touchstone of musical validity whether it manifests itself in Britten or the Beatles. For many people, the further music diverges from known and understood harmonies and rhythms, the less valid it becomes. In the final analysis, the validity of anything must depend upon a certain level of acceptance from 'users'. There can be no doubt that musical values relating to texture, colour, density etc. are gaining wider acceptance and it may be felt by a music teacher that it is part of his job at least to introduce some of these new sounds to his classes. If that duty is valid then the validity of the activity is implied, if only on educational grounds. The results may not be acceptable generally as music, but at least the choice is offered. The individuals in the class can form their own conclusions based on what they are doing and hearing. So the answer to the first question is arrived at: the class is being taught to develop discernment and to explore beyond generally held assumptions.

Conclusion

Singing is a basis for a wide variety of musical activities. As with so much teaching, clear objectives will lead to purposeful activity. The teacher is the expert. He knows in which department his pupils need help, practice and instruction. If we look back at the sixth use of singing in education – singing is an easy way of filling up a music lesson – we can see how much can be lost by pulling the song-books off the shelf, passing them around the class and asking for 'requests'. I feel sure that time-filling diversions of this sort offer little fulfilment to anyone in the long run. Having taught like that myself at one time, I was forced to look for new approaches, to think about the reasons for singing being part of music education at all.

Lesson plans

The two lesson plans below are for the teaching of vocal technique in one case and musical literacy in the other. The same song is used in both lessons.

Lesson Plan 1
Objective: By the end of the lesson the children will have improved their singing techniques.
Enabling Objective: By the end of the lesson the children will have developed their breath control and be able to sing higher notes securely and with a good tone.
Equipment: Words for 'You are my Sunshine' (*Ta-ra-ra Boom-de-ay*, p. 16).
Introduction: Teach song by rote, phrase by phrase, without piano accompaniment.
Development: Pinpoint phrasing and relate to breathing.
Two short phrases: 'The other night dear'
                  'As I lay dreaming'
One long phrase: 'I dreamt that you were by my side'
Teach correct breathing (i.e. from the diaphragm) for more efficient management of the long phrase. Concentrate on 'Came disillusion . . .'.
Explain use of the head voice for upper notes and practise.
Develop these features in the remainder of the song.
Conclusion: Sing whole song (two verses) with piano accompaniment.

Lesson Plan 2
Objective: By the end of the lesson the children will have enlarged their capacity to read music.
Enabling Objective: By the end of the lesson the children will be able to understand what a tie is in music and will begin to grasp the significance of the sharp sign.
Equipment: Two copies of 'You are my Sunshine', one with the words written beneath the notes and one without; small drum.
Introduction: Distribute wordless copies. Having explained the tie, play through the song on the piano with the children following. Stop unexpectedly and ask for bearings. When it is apparent that the children can follow the song, play through non-stop.
Development: Give further explanation of the tie and reasons for its existence.

Demonstrate by asking one child to maintain a regular crotchet pulse on a drum while the tied note continues over the bar line. Sing the song to lah. Ensure that all the variants of tied notes are covered. (The song contains three different ties spread over thirteen examples.)

Draw attention to the G sharp in bar 3. Play the tune with a G natural and then again with a G sharp. Sing in the same manner. Explain tones and semitones, using this as an example.

Conclusion: Sing through the song from the sheet with words.

You are my sunshine

The other night, dear,
As I lay dreaming,
I dreamt that you were by my side.
Came disillusion
When I awoke, dear,
You were gone and then I cried.

I'll always love you
And make you happy,
If you will only do the same.
But if you leave me,
How it will grieve me;
Nevermore I'll breathe your name.

You are my sunshine,
My only sunshine,
You make me happy
When skies are grey,
You'll never know, dear,
How much I love you;
Please don't take my sunshine away.

Words and music by Jimmie Davis and Charles Mitchell
© Copyright 1940 by PEER INTERNATIONAL CORPORATION, 1619 Broadway,
New York 19, N.Y.
© Copyright 1957 by PEER INTERNATIONAL CORPORATION, 1619 Broadway,
New York 19, N.Y.
Southern Music Publishing Co., Ltd., 8, Denmark St. London

5 INSTRUMENTAL MUSIC IN THE CLASSROOM

Those alliterative antagonists, process and product, have lain at the centre of many educational debates, and, not least, of those in music education. The debate itself is a process, and its product is sometimes little more than furrowed brows and confused thoughts. If the act of preparing music, the process, has been absorbing, does it really matter what the end result, the product, sounds like? If the end result is unimpressive, does it not imply that the preparation has been a waste of time? What balance should be aimed for between these ill-matched claims for attention? Having taken part in discussion of this sort with appropriate earnestness, I have come to the conclusion that the issue is something of a bubble. The more important issue in music education is whether to make music or not. If the decision is *not* to make music, then there is no issue left to resolve. If the decision *is* to make music, then likewise, the issue has disappeared. Once the decision to make music has been taken, the philosophical agonising can come to an end. I have seen children delighted with and deeply involved in polishing a recorder piece (product), in learning to improvise over an ostinato (process), in performing a suite of classroom orchestra pieces (product) and in experimenting with a piano-harp (process). How absurd it is to condemn any of these activities because of a label. In this chapter I shall concern myself with both aspects of musical activity without distinction because, as far as they can be separated clearly, both contribute towards musical experience and achievement.

I have chosen five kinds of instrumental music-making for close scrutiny. They are the percussion band, recorder playing, Orff-Schulwerk, music-making in pop and rock idioms and the classroom orchestra. Creative music-making is discussed in chapter 6. The boundaries between the categories are blurred at times; indeed, to experienced teachers, such pigeon-holing could seem artificial since a course of instrumental playing may contain a mixture of methods, impossible to unscramble. Despite this, each of the five approaches is distinctive and it is easier to make an evaluation of any one of them when it is seen in an unadulterated, if slightly unreal, form.

The five practices are looked at separately and, after that, each is considered in relation to the three principles set out in chapter 2, and then alongside considerations of musical literacy, timbre and idiom. The chapter ends with two sample lesson plans of instrumental music-making in class.

The percussion band

My first experience of group music-making was in a percussion band. I was about six years old and I loved it. I can picture myself, a fattish little boy with podgy knock-knees protruding from long grey flannel shorts. On my face is an expression of intense concentration as I wait my turn to strike a triangle held aloft in my left hand with a six-inch nail clutched in my right. I understand the notation and Miss Kemp plays the piano with tremendously helpful emphasis even though the music is called 'Sunset on the River'. At that age I enjoyed everything at school but I longed for percussion band. I delighted in learning to read music, in playing rhythmically and in the intoxicating crashes and thumps of our eager, infant efforts. What a fortunate thing it was that I had not read the literature on percussion band at that tender age! Had I done so, I would have been filled with disappointment. The emotion which should have gripped me was the love of good music. All the writers said so from Marie Salt in 1914 ('Music and the Young Child', in S. Macpherson and E. Reed, *Aural Culture based upon Musical Appreciation*, 2nd edn, Joseph Williams) to Yvonne Adair in 1952. My own feelings about reading and playing music were not nearly so important. It was Handel's (or any other composer's) thoughts which mattered. Through our noisy overlay, the goodness of Handel's music should come through unscathed and enter our bloodstreams. If I could extend my arm backwards in time, I would give that child a pat on the head as if to say: 'You're really enjoying yourself, aren't you? Forget about what the books say.' I feel certain that I would have enjoyed the percussion band regardless of the music being played. It was the thrill of involvement which moved me, not the goodness of the music. I can think of no better way of giving young children a real experience of playing music. It instils awareness on so many levels and behind it lies a wealth of material to use.

Yvonne Adair's book, *Music through the Percussion Band*, offers a fully structured course and discusses the instruments to use, organisation of forces and indeed all a teacher needs to know. Though one is inclined, perhaps, to associate automatically the percussion band with infant children, there have been examples of high success in the medium with secondary school classes. The heyday of the percussion band was between the world wars and an indication of its use with older children is found in the Paxton School Percussion Series Catalogue which included an arrangement of the whole of Brahms' Symphony no. 4. Though largely superseded by recorders, Orff-Schulwerk and more recent developments, the percussion band still has much to offer at all levels of education. For instance:

It is capable of being well structured.

By ignoring matters of pitch, progress can be rapid.

There are parts well suited to the less able.

Instruments are generally cheap to buy and often in the school already.

However, there are drawbacks to the activity:

Rhythm education flies ahead of pitch education, leaving an unnatural gap in the children's musical awareness and knowledge.

The sound is unvaried.

The teacher must be a good pianist or use a colleague to play the piano or else depend on recordings. The percussion band barely stands on its own.

It is possibly a coincidence that, as the traditional percussion band declined, a new form was introduced. *New Sounds in Class* by George Self was published in 1967. In his compositions, conventional pulse is abandoned altogether, precise instructions concerning timbre are relaxed and the melodic rôle of the piano is dispensed with. Using grids of graphic notation, Self has written pieces which emerge, in effect, as 'instant' avant-garde music, the emphasis being placed on the juxtaposition of textures, the general tessitura of instrumental capabilities, the colour of sounds, the modes of attack or articulation and dynamics. In the book, symbols on horizontal parallel lines show the players the kind of sound expected (e.g. short or long, quiet or soft), while vertical lines, which are numbered, indicate the passing of time. A conductor merely signals the arrival of each vertical line, whereupon appropriate action is taken by the players. The sounds are indeed 'new' to most children. There is little room for improvisation or invention, but, even so, two performances of one piece might vary widely due to a different selection of instruments and different timings by the conductors. There are other, similar publications available and there is much scope for children to devise their own pieces on the same lines. Despite differences in idiom, there are points of kinship between new and traditional percussion-band work. In both, the players use percussion instruments. In both, they must 'get it right' by making the right kind of sound at the right time. Both are structured and graded.

A curious feature of the British educational system is that schools enjoy great autonomy in matters of curriculum. Some subjects, music being a notable example, flourish in one school and languish in the next. If music as a classroom subject is in its infancy in any school, the percussion band, old style or new style, might well prove to be the ideal springboard for fruitful development.

Recorder playing

What is more lovely than a solitary pipe playing 'Greensleeves' on a mountain-side? And what is more excruciating than thirty pipes trying to play the same tune in a classroom? This is the dilemma of the recorder as an educational instrument. Of all the educational instruments it is the only 'real' one. It has a rich literature and distinguished executants. It has a sturdy construction and no mechanism and it is cheap to buy. With all these advantages it should be ideal, but thirty players, some unwilling, some inept, and all with strong lungs, make us think twice before embarking upon a course of recorder tuition in class.

Yet some teachers achieve great success with the instrument. It appears that once the initial stages have been mastered, the work can settle down quickly. Pleasant sounds can begin to emerge. If the first hurdles are crucial to success, it is these which should be examined closely.

There are electronic organs which, provided the right stops are depressed, will play an attractive if well-worn chord sequence with decorative arpeggios and discreet rhythmic accompaniment *ad nauseam*. All the player has to do is to press the 'on' switch. The novelty of this expensive toy, like that of cheaper ones, will wear thin unless it is associated with some sense of achievement on the part of its owner. However, the germ of a message is present for recorder teachers. The organ is producing real music immediately. It creates an illusion that the hard grind of learning can be dispensed with. Of course it cannot, but we are reminded that hard grind by itself might suggest that real music can be dispensed with – the direct opposite of the electronic organ. This is what many first recorder lessons appear to be: hard grind and no music. When parents buy their child a clarinet or a trumpet, they often expect to hear a tune after the first lesson. When a teacher puts thirty recorders into thirty pairs of hands, he generally does not expect to hear a tune. The children, on the other hand, do, and so often the first lesson becomes a lesson in disillusionment: hard grind and no music.

Whereas percussion band activities are easy to get off the ground because considerations of technique and pitch reading are absent, the first recorder lesson could be spent trying to master and understand five different things culminating in the modest achievement of one note being played:

The fingering for B
The naming of the note B
The reading of the pitch of the note B
The reading of the length of the note B
The articulation (tonguing) of the note B

Of these scraps of skill and knowledge, one only is essential – the fingering. The name can wait, the reading can wait, and articulation will look after itself for the time being.

I have seen an exciting lesson where the note B formed the basis for real musical experience. Instead of using drills and exercises which immediately shift the focus of the lesson from experience to knowledge, the teacher taught the fingering for B and then started to improvise on the piano in E major, occasionally visiting E minor, G major and other keys where the note B can be telling and expressive. 'Come on. Join in!' he called to the class and very quickly a regular crotchet beat emerged naturally from all thirty players – a most attractive swarm of Bs. Curiously, the old problems of overblowing and misfingerings did not arise because the coarseness and sharpness caused through overblowing were so obvious, the children were unwilling to spoil their own delight. With only one fingering to think about, there could be no misfingering. Following this success, the teacher taught the fingering for A. He played short rhythmic phrases on the recorder using A and B and the children imitated. He turned his back on the class so that they had to base their imitation on what they heard, not on what they saw. He then returned to the piano and improvised again, this time in G major, shifting from tonic to dominant with unadorned regularity. The class joined in. Soon, the more able children grasped the message and moved from B to A and back again, synchronising with the changes of harmony in the piano playing. The rest of the class picked it up and the musical result was vital and mesmeric. In the few remaining minutes of the lesson, the teacher gave the names of the notes and wrote them up on the manuscript blackboard. The children were interested and ready for more.

For me, the lesson demonstrated perfectly the maxim of all celebrated music educationalists from Pestalozzi to Kodály: sound first, sign second. Of course notation is vital in music where written notes are used and as a foundation for future progress, but our way into music (or perhaps I should say music's way into us) is through sound, not dots.

The third note to establish on the recorder is G. Some teachers start with G and move upwards through A to B. The use of three fingers requires more skill than the use of one, so the sequence B, A, G may be regarded always as the most effective. There are not many tunes using these three notes only, but there are some. (See appendix for details.) With appropriate harmonic accompaniment, a fairly characterless line of notes can be given a convincing sense of direction. By this stage, some children are ready to leap ahead. They have acquired a feeling for the instrument and seem to have little difficulty in remembering fingerings and reading notation. Others struggle. To reach the lower holes, they may move their left hand down the instrument rather than use the right. They may develop the infuriating knack of never being able to cover all the holes tightly, the leaks causing aberrant noises of all sorts. To accommodate the able and the less able within one lesson is a challenge. The introduction of two-part material is one useful solution, while a move towards a more varied ensemble – the addition of untuned percussion etc. – is another.

Most children can master five notes on a recorder but there is a difference of opinion as to which five notes should be learned. B, A and G are accepted as being the first three of the five. The addition of low E and low D completes a pentatonic scale, thus fitting in well with Orff-Schulwerk. (See below.) It also avoids cross-fingerings. However, it uses six fingers and a thumb, which requires a fairly high level of co-ordination. The lower notes need especially gentle use of the breath. The alternative to low E and D is the addition of the C and D above B, thus creating the first five notes of an ascending G major scale. The advantages here are that only three fingers and a thumb are used and that there is plenty of music available within this compass. However, cross-fingerings from B to C or from B to D can call for a great deal of patient practice.

The choice must rest on the type of work or textbook being used. Kenneth Simpson's excellent *Music through the Recorder* favours the low E and D while all other reputable tutors favour the high C and D. Improvisatory work is more effective with the lower notes and the lower tessitura is less wearing on the ear.

If the lower scheme is used, Brocklehurst's *Pentatonic Songbooks* offer material some of which can be transposed for recorders with good effect. For the upper scheme, Winters' *Pleasure and Practice with the Recorder, Book 1* contains nineteen tunes within the compass. My own series, *Class in Concert*, contains twenty-three. A further twenty-four will be found in *Duo Kits* 1–4. (See appendix.)

In mixed-ability classes where all the children are expected to play the recorder, ambitious stretching beyond five notes is inclined to founder. Some children are unable to develop their manual skills or reading abilities further. The house of cards collapses, so to speak, and a frustrated child with a recorder in his hands can be disruptive. However, by using two-part material or by broadening the ensemble, the more able children can advance. All the established tutors for recorder move optimistically forward to quite dizzy heights. While some children tackle the advanced work, the less able can play a more simple counterpoint composed by the teacher.

Orff-Schulwerk

Carl Orff, the German composer, described his Method as being 'creative'. If improvisation and varied imitation may be regarded as being creative, then his description stands. However, there is no suggestion that the children should be given sufficient creative freedom to influence the course of work in any drastic way. Rather, the teacher, working in accordance with the Method, enlarges an area which the children may explore musically. There is freedom, but always within clearly understood limits. These limits are extended little by little as the concepts and skills are grasped. The element of creativity is not sufficiently dominant for individual contributions to show great character.

At the beginning, when the area is most restricted, the Method resembles closely that of Kodály. Indeed, it is, first of all, a method embracing vocal and instrumental music-making together with physical movement. In Britain, it is the instrumental aspects of Orff-Schulwerk which have received most attention, but it must be stressed that the uses of language and simple body sounds are fundamental to the Method, even when the heaviest concentration is being placed upon the instrumental work.

Like Kodály, Orff starts the rhythmic training with the names of children and everyday words. These are chanted rhythmically, treated in canon and set against each other, inculcating a firm traditional sense of pulse.

Moving away from words, the Method transfers the rhythms to body sounds: clapping, finger-snapping, *patschen* (knee-slapping) and foot-stamping. Through gesture, the teacher can indicate variations in dynamic and tempo. From this grow 'question and answer' sessions. The teacher presents a short rhythmic figure, using body sounds. The children imitate either as a class or individually. This extends to answers from single pupils which can diverge from the question. They need no longer imitate exactly but can make up variations within the prevailing rhythmic framework. They are starting to explore. In order to maintain a steady pulse throughout the exercise, one child can play an ostinato, perhaps on an unpitched instrument like a tambour or else on a pitched instrument such as a bass xylophone.

As in the Kodály Method, pitch is first introduced through the falling minor third, but here sol-fa is not used. The work is predominantly aural, standard notation being introduced at a much later stage. Two bars of a pitched percussion instrument are left intact on an otherwise stripped carcass. The question and answer games are continued through percussion work, again over an ostinato. The range of notes extends to the use of the pentatonic scale and, in many schools, gets no further than that. However, Orff's Method moves on to major and minor scales and to rhythms of considerable complexity. Simple formal devices such as the rondo are employed with improvised episodes forming an important part of the whole.

This description has been brief because there is literature available which explains every detail. The most complete manual is Keetman's *Elementaria* but Hall's teacher's manual for the Canadian version of Orff-Schulwerk is more succinct and possibly serves as a more useful introduction. Orff himself, with Keetman, produced five volumes of music, *Music for Children*, which seem to conflict with notions of improvisation and creativity. They are fully-scored pieces covering the ideas in the Method from beginning to end. They could either be performed in a purely re-creative way or else be used as models for improvisatory work.

There are many manifestations of Orff-Schulwerk. It is a shame that Orff himself wrote so little about his scheme of music-making by children. Orff-Schulwerk societies have sprung up in many countries and the literature is voluminous. It is hardly surprising that the research and devotion has thrown up more problems than solutions. Should the work begin with infants or can a teacher start at secondary level if he so chooses? Can the recorder be included in the early stages. Does the music have to remain diatonic and four-square in time? Is a teacher allowed to make Orff-Schulwerk part of his course or is the choice 'all or nothing'?

It seems that some teachers regard the mere fact of using 'Orff' instruments as being indicative of pursuing a course of Orff-Schulwerk. Clearly, such a view cannot be accepted without question, but, on the other hand, Orff-Schulwerk is not sufficiently defined for us to state categorically whether any particular piece of work is within or beyond the pale. However, if barred percussion instruments dominate the texture, if ostinati and simple rondo, ternary and variation forms are used, and if melodies are predominantly repetitive and diatonic, we may be sure that Orff's influence is at work, whether the music be part of a structured course or an isolated project.

All classroom sounds (percussion band, recorders, classroom orchestra) are, to a greater or lesser extent, restricted. Orff-Schulwerk is especially restricted for four main reasons. Firstly, the instruments used are mainly those of the pitched percussion family: glockenspiels, xylophones and metallophones. The continuous, often slightly unsynchronised clunking of beaters against bars can be wearing. Secondly, the metre, once established, can be relentless, especially in the earlier stages of the work. Thirdly, the use of ostinato, though helpful as an anchor and as a formal device, can be suggestive of hamsters scampering unproductively in millwheels. Finally, the pentatonic scale is limited from an expressive point of view and of doubtful validity as a framework for improvisatory work. True, there is never a clash of a semitone, but the absence of such a pitfall (if pitfall it is) can lead to a somewhat arbitrary choice of notes and a sneaking doubt in the listener's mind as to whether some children have learned the rules of a game they do not understand.

These criticisms are severe but seem to be shared by many music teachers. Orff-Schulwerk as a *Method* has never been widespread in this country. Nevertheless, the early stages, particularly those concerning rhythm training and improvisation, are ingenious and useful and can lead to exciting work in other areas such as the blues and mixed ensemble work.

Making music in pop and rock idioms

Most of the literature on pop music in education is concerned with either presentation of pop music as listening material or schemes of written work *about* pop music. (I use 'pop' as a word of convenience to cover jazz, rock, pop and other music derived from Afro-American idioms.) Few writers have dared to grasp the nettle of making pop music in class, yet this is an activity which can unburden pop music of one of its great shortcomings – the once and for all artifact enshrined on a disc. How often is one able to hear two interpretations of the same song? Very rarely. The freezing of a performance and its attendant over-exposure can create a consensus that music is solely a spectator sport. In class, the children can put something of themselves into the idiom. The music can come alive and the waxwork of petrified emotions that constitutes so much of the commercial output is forgotten, at least for the time being. This is not to suggest that the children open their books at page 17 and sing a current pop song. Their involvement can be more creative than that.

Of the exponents of making pop music in class Piers Spencer is one of the most articulate and organised. His chapters in *Pop Music in School* edited by Vulliamy and Lee are explicit in two areas. The first deals with the construction of instrumental and vocal Blues while the second branches out into freer composition. A cassette accompanies the book. Short though the chapters are, they provide enough impetus to set a teacher going, provided he has a sympathy and feeling for the idiom.

It will be seen from Spencer's work that structure plays an important rôle. The Orff-derived ostinati or riffs form the basis for increasingly elaborate composition and improvisation. Each time the children are given freedom to experiment, it is within a thoroughly understood framework, always based on previously learned skills and concepts. So secure is this foundation, the question of idiom diminishes in importance. So obviously are the children involved in their work, questions as to whether pop music is the child's natural milieu or an abomination matched only by bubble gum and space invaders seem irrelevant. The value of structured musical experience is the great gain. The style of the experience becomes a subsidiary issue.

The twelve-bar Blues chord sequence is a fine vehicle for improvisation in class. It is sufficiently varied to dissipate the relentless repetition found in so much Orff-Schulwerk yet simple enough to be understood by most children. There are several variants of the Blues found in *Pop Music in School*. An instrumental refrain for the whole class, in which an unadorned statement of the sequence predominates, can alternate with vocal or instrumental solos accompanied by piano, drums and bass guitar.

Spencer alludes to the advantages of using an electric bass guitar and a drumkit in the classroom. The shrill voices of recorders, the jangling of glockenspiels and the thump of toy drums share the lack of a sturdy foundation. The presence of a bass guitar goes a long way to rectify the imbalance. Similarly, a drumkit, even in the hands of a slightly experienced player, serves as a vital rhythmic bond. Both instruments can be used in other forms of music-making, notably in the classroom orchestra.

Classroom orchestra

Classroom orchestra grows out of much of what has been covered in this chapter so far and more besides. If the store cupboard contains unpitched and pitched percussion instruments, some recorders, a few violins, some guitars and maybe harmonicas and melodicas, the obvious development is to use them together as an elementary orchestra. Many classes contain their specialists – children who are learning orchestral instruments or guitars. These people can be incorporated into the ensemble as well. There are decisions and compromises to be made in order to combine these disparate forces together satisfactorily.

The day-to-day running of a classroom orchestra has been discussed in chapter 3. The character of the music and the development of musical skills and literacy will depend upon decisions made before a note has been played. Below is an account of my thoughts and actions. Anyone intending to write their own material for classroom orchestra might find the questions I asked useful starting points in their own planning. Their answers could turn out to be very different from mine.

I was fortunate in being bequeathed a good collection of classroom instruments by previous music teachers at my first school. All I needed in addition was music. I decided to write my own and, as a first step, made enquiries as to what instrumentalists were present in each class. Here are the lists for two of them:

2A (30 children): 8 descant recorders, 1 treble recorder, 2 clarinets, 1 violin,

1 flute, 1 guitar. The remaining 16 played nothing.

3A (28 children): 4 descant recorders, 3 clarinets, 1 'cello, 1 trumpet, 1 euphonium, 1 trombone. The remaining 17 played nothing.

I was delighted with this unusual wealth of skill and during an evening composed two pieces, one for each class. The non-specialists were to play glockenspiels, harmonicas (of which the school possessed a large stock) and unpitched percussion.

Both compositions were successful. The close parallel harmony I had devised for the descant and treble recorders in 2A delighted us all while the euphonium solo which I had used as a counterpoint to a sombre chorale-like melody for clarinets, 'cello and trombone was thought by my kind pupils in 3A to be a model of ingenuity. We worked hard at the pieces for a few weeks, performed them in assembly and then embarked upon some more pieces which I had prepared in anticipation. The new music was a little more difficult to read and play but was equally successful.

This pattern of work continued for a term or two. Other classes started on classroom orchestra work. They had yet further unusual instrumental groupings and the proliferation of tailor-made compositions caused me to think afresh.

If 2A's music was to be used by 2B it would have to be rescored. I could avoid this labour by contriving a compromise score – one which could serve the requirements of any class. I decided to use five 'classroom' instruments. They were descant (or tenor) recorder, harmonica, tuned percussion, open-string violin and untuned percussion. One of my classes contained no specialist players, so the entire sound was created by groups of these five instruments together with piano accompaniment. However, the school was rich in instrumentalists and I wondered how to incorporate them into the group without resorting to a score of unmanageable proportions. Some drastic compromises were needed. The violins, oboes and flutes could join the recorders. All are instruments in C and all play from the treble clef. (The more advanced violinists and flautists played the music an octave higher.) I created a B flat part for clarinets, trumpets and cornets and a bass line for all the orchestral bass instruments: bassoon, trombone, tuba, 'cello and double bass. For the guitarists I constructed a part asking for appropriate chords. Four groups were omitted from my scheme: treble recorders, violas, french horns and the low-pitched brass band instruments. When players of these instruments were present in the class, I would prepare a part for them. Very few groups contained specialists enough for the whole score to be covered, so the sound varied from one class to the next and my piano playing had to take on a new level of versatility.

The Score

Line 1: Descant and tenor recorders, violin, flute, oboe

Line 2: Harmonica

Line 3: Tuned percussion

Line 4: Easy violin

Line 5: Untuned percussion

Line 6: (In B flat) clarinet, trumpet, cornet
Line 7: Guitar
Line 8: Bassoon, trombone, tuba, 'cello, double bass
Line 9: Piano

It was the establishment of this 'standard' score which allowed me to experiment in other areas. I had taught musical literacy at an elementary level through singing and recorder playing prior to embarking upon classroom orchestra work, so I knew pretty well what level of understanding most of the pupils would show. I knew that genuine music reading by most children needs 'props'. I contained my urge to write subtle rhythms and flowing counterpoints. A few children would grasp them but most would not. The best rhythmic prop in the introductory pieces would be the requirement of all the players to play the *same* rhythm. The weak could follow the strong. Even this simplification needed some structuring. The limited material available at that time (e.g. *Group Music Making* by McMurtary, Longman, 1972) seemed to me to use too wide a range of rhythmic symbols. A glance at a few folksongs shows that most melodies use a ratio of notelengths of 1:4. If the shortest note is a quaver then the longest is a minim which is four times a quaver. If the shortest note is a crotchet then the longest is a semibreve. Some tunes use a ratio of 1:8, i.e. quaver to semibreve, but very few indeed use 1:16. I decided that my compositions for classroom orchestra would use the 1:4 ratio and extend to 1:8 when the time was ripe. This decision ruled out the need to teach quavers in the first instance and the need ever to teach semiquavers. These restrictions did not apply to the piano part which I generally played myself.

Because all players played the same rhythm, their rhythmic education was uniform. However, the pupils' progress in matters of instrumental technique and pitch education was bound to vary, so I worked out a scheme for each instrument, hoping that the understanding of a recorder player, for instance, would keep pace with that of a glockenspiel player. The lines of development I conceived were as follows:

Recorders

I decided upon G, A, B, C, D as the five main notes to establish in preference to the pentatonic Low D, Low E, G, A, B. The lower notes could be problematical for beginner flautists and oboists who also played this line. To start with, I devised melodies with a high proportion of adjacent notes and a minimum of cross-fingerings (e.g. B to C) and widened the range only much later in the course, the lower right hand notes first and then the upper octave along with chromatic notes. I always wrote letter names beneath the notes to assist the weaker readers.

Harmonicas

We used diatonic instruments pitched in C. Using the letters B for 'blow' and S for 'suck', the harmonica is played as follows:

Middle	C	D	E	F	G	A	B	C
	B1	S1	B2	S2	B3	S3	S4	B4 or B5

The numbers are engraved over the holes on leading makes of the instrument. The second octave follows the same pattern starting with 'B5'. By writing playing instructions into the part, I felt I gave the players a chance to tackle the music with confidence. In all of the early pieces, I confined the part to one hole so that the children need not become confused by the movement of the instrument across the mouth, and never did I use more than the first three holes. With less-able children, the melodica proved useful on this part. With only two keys to press, they soon felt a sense of accomplishment. I also used chime bars on occasion.

Tuned percussion

I learned quickly that these instruments are not so easy to play. Even with the letter names written underneath the notes in the part (they are also marked on the instruments), the children would scan their glockenspiels and xylophones, searching desperately for the note needed, the beater hovering like a fly swat. The cause of the difficulty was twofold. Firstly, I was inclined to leave too large gaps between notes. For beginners, adjacent or near adjacent notes are much easier to cope with. Secondly, I learned to my astonishment that many pupils were weak alphabetically. They barely knew that F abutted G. If the music included a descending phrase, it was worse because the alphabet then ran backwards. At the beginning, I kept the music towards the right-hand end of the instrument so that the notes could be located easily. As the course progressed, I moved towards the middle and spread the notes out more.

Easy violin

This part was included because there were violins not being used and it struck me that they could make a small but noticeable contribution. The part used open strings only and I taught the players to hold the instrument banjo-fashion, plucking the strings with their right hand thumbs. Later they changed to the conventional under-the-chin position. Some of them moved on to tackling the use of the bow and by the end of my course I was asking them to play notes with the first finger of the left hand besides the open strings. I was not particularly concerned about 'correct' technique, since none of the players would be taking up the instrument as a serious extra-curricular study.

Untuned percussion

There were no problems of pitch here, of course, so I encouraged the players to read the music 'straight' and then to improvise their contributions in ways which matched the mood of the music.

B flat part

The 'Rubicon' for beginners on the clarinet is the manoeuvre from B flat to B natural in the stave. Known as 'the break', it involves a high degree of co-ordination and most clarinet teachers tackle the problem only when the lower register is secure. Because most of my clarinet players were at the elementary stages of learning, I kept the part below B, i.e. below the break. Fortunately, this suited the beginners on trumpets and cornets as well, B flat serving as a comfortable upper limit. In due course, I split the B flat part, allowing the upper one to explore the region lying above the break.

Guitar

A number of my pupils could strum a guitar and it seemed a waste not to make use of their talents. I decided to include in the ensemble a guitar part consisting of chords. The more able players could devise right-hand configurations where and when it seemed appropriate. I found immediately that the harmonies I chose to suit the capabilities of the other instruments in the ensemble did not necessarily suit logical progress on the guitar. I was unwilling, unable often, to make fundamental alterations to the music, so I tackled the problem from the performance end. Using a number of guitarists, I taught each player one chord in the first instance. They locked their fingers into position and played only when their particular chord was needed. Over the weeks I changed them about, so gradually, each guitarist built up a repertoire of chords. On one occasion I tried to tune each guitar to a different chord, so that an idle strum with the right hand would produce automatically the chord required. I abandoned this expedient after breaking two strings.

The bass line

Many of my classes contained no bass instrument, but when a bass instrument was present, I found it most valuable. The parts I wrote were straightforward because of the varying problems on the different instruments. For instance, low B is easy enough on a 'cello but a challenge for a short-armed trombonist. When possible, I used a bass xylophone on this part, and I have found that an electric bass guitar makes a marked improvement to the overall sound.

The use of key

Once I had decided to confine my recorder part to five notes, I imposed upon myself the challenge of writing original tunes rather than making arrangements. The recorder line carried the main weight of melodic interest, so the notes G, A, B, C and D were the ingredients for many recipes. Even though I had decided to write my own tunes, I thought it worthwhile to examine well-known melodies which were equally confined in range. I studied the recorder manuals in particular and noticed that the overwhelming majority of the tunes were in G major. This is because folk melodies (which is what most of them were) must stand on their own. Their harmony is implied and, as a result, G becomes the tonic and D the dominant. It struck me that with classroom orchestra new approaches would be available since the harmonies are more than implied; they are actually there. Consequently, I treated the key of G major with caution. It seemed to me to be a much overworked key in school instrumental music. I explored possibilities in C major, A minor, E minor and various modes. Later I ventured into F major and B flat major, using B natural as a chromatic decoration, avoiding B flat altogether.

The tessitura of the melodies

Another difficulty arising through the restriction of five notes is that of melodic direction. Very quickly the tune can lose impetus. It can seem to be going nowhere in particular. My way round this problem was to hold a note back, at least from a strong beat, so that when it did emerge, it produced an air of freshness and lifted the tune on to a new plane.

Idiom

Every idiom is inclusive and exclusive at the same time. Major chords are often out of place in avant-garde music while chord clusters rarely suit Christmas carols. I was anxious to avoid automatic associations with the work I was doing in classroom orchestra. Nursery songs have attractive tunes well suited to the technical requirements of the course, but I was in little doubt that a good number of these big children would reject the chance to re-live their infanthood in this way. I also thought, possibly wrongly, that they would reject pop-orientated music, since the results could be only a shadow of the originals. In improvisatory work in pop and rock idioms, some authenticity can be suggested through the use of complex rhythms. Such complexities are no special problem in aurally based work. Where the music is being read, however, the written notes must of necessity be simple and restricted. Because most pop melodies require notation which would baffle the average recorder player, I was strong in my resolve to write fresh material and avoid arrangements. Though the results were like nursery rhymes in many cases, the children raised no objections. They were too deeply immersed in what they were doing to bother about matters of style and cultural association.

The teacher's rôle in classroom orchestra

Classroom orchestra appears to be a typical teacher-directed activity. It is the baby brother of the professional orchestra. The rehearsal procedures, outlined in chapter 3, apply in essence to any orchestral rehearsal. However, in classroom orchestra, there is more to achieve than a polished performance. Whereas in a professional orchestra the conductor is moulding the skills of his players into a presentable end-product, a teacher is doing the same and building up musical literacy and instrumental expertise besides. He must teach as well as rehearse and the balance between the two duties is a matter for fine judgement.

But a teacher is not compelled to be the juggler implied by the above. He can, as an alternative, allow elements of experiment and discovery to enter his scheme. Creative activities in the music room have demonstrated that groupwork, far from providing a recipe for disorder, is an effective way of learning through trial and error and through flashes of insight. In two ways, such group activity can be used in classroom orchestra work, provided there is space available.

Firstly, the children can be instructed to work at their parts in sectional groups. Having explained basic rhythms and fingerings to the class as a whole, the teacher sets the children to sort out problems and polish their contributions in groups. The recorder players work in one corner of the room while the tuned percussion players work in another, and so on. After passing from group to group, helping to solve intractable difficulties, he brings them back together as an orchestra and welds the various units of independent work into a unity.

The other place for groupwork is in the field of 'chamber music'. Once the class is familiar with the styles and procedures of classroom orchestra, they can be grouped into smaller mixed ensembles, each being given the task of preparing one piece of music for performance. The culmination of this activity would be an intimate concert where each group in turn presents its work to the rest of the class. An activity of this sort can build up a sense of musical responsibility in each child. Other, more inventive, possibilities are discussed in chapter 6.

Some comparisons

I hope the comparisons I make will be thought of as commodious rather than odious. There can be no doubt that all of the instrumental activities covered in this chapter contribute towards children's musical experience and sense of achievement, but how well do they measure up against the three principles spelled out in chapter 2? And what about the questions of musical literacy, timbre and idiom, mentioned earlier? I feel that all of these are major considerations and the somewhat clinical approach used below may help others in deciding where to orientate their instrumental work in the classroom.

First principle: The work must be suitable for the majority of pupils in the class

Percussion band

Suits everyone well. The less able can play simpler parts.

Recorders

Most classes contain some children who find even two notes on a recorder difficult to play. However, patient and skilful teaching can instil at least three notes and generally five. Beyond this point, the activity becomes less acceptable for full classes of children.

Orff-Schulwerk

Orff insisted that no child was unmusical and devised his scheme so that every child could participate. His Method can include every talent, however modest.

Pop and Rock

Very similar to Orff-Schulwerk. There is no Method, as such, as it is up to the teacher to ensure that the work remains at a level suited to all the children.

Classroom orchestra

The wide choice of instruments gives the teacher a chance to use every person in accordance with his capabilities. The simplicity of the notation makes the activity thoroughly accessible.

Second principle: Music in the classroom should be an active, participatory subject

All the approaches fulfil this principle.

Third principle: The activities in the music classroom should be organised into structured courses of study

Percussion band

Both old and new forms of percussion-band work can be organised into structured courses.

Recorders

There are several courses available. All of them are methodical. Some of them move forward too quickly and supplementary material would have to be devised.

Orff-Schulwerk

If *Music for Children* is a model, this is the most structured scheme of all. However, the shape and direction of the course rests on the teacher's decisions and careful forethought is needed in order to preserve logical progress.

Pop and rock

Spencer's work is an example of a structured course within this field. It is most unlikely that success could be obtained without methodical approaches of this sort.

Classroom orchestra

Class in Concert is closely structured. A framework for a course of work on similar lines has been outlined in these pages.

Musical literacy

Though some children enjoy learning notation, especially when it is linked with practical activity, others do not. A mixture of these children is bound to be present in nearly every class. The purpose of notation in classwork is to help children to make music. It seems purposeless to make music in order to learn notation. If we have to make end-of-term assessments, the tests should provide an answer to the question: 'Can this child make music?', not: 'Can this child read music?' When the children need to read in order to play or sing, then we must test reading abilities, but only in relation to the singing and playing. A child who can understand musical theory but who cannot put it to musical use, has been educated in a distorted manner.

The need to be literate musically should not be thought of as being a question of principle. If an activity suffers from a doctrinaire insistence on literacy, or, conversely, suffers from a doctrinaire insistence on the avoidance of literacy, it must suffer. There is no need to crack a nut with a sledge-hammer, but, on the other hand, we should think carefully before eschewing the advantages of nutcrackers.

Percussion band

Literacy is central to percussion-band work. Whether it be with toy instruments ranged round a piano or the 'new sounds' of George Self, success depends upon faithfulness to the written page. Because of the structured approaches used, the problems are minimised and the challenges of reading enhance rather than diminish the pleasures of participation. The literacy acquired is of a restricted nature. In traditional activities it is confined to rhythmic symbols only, while in the avant-garde work, precise symbols of pitch and time are absent altogether. Because of this, the children are not well-equipped to tackle other forms of music-making which depend upon musical literacy.

Recorders

As the work with recorders advances, so too does the emphasis on reading ability. Indeed, the minutiae of musical literacy can cause the activity to grind to a halt. I know of no approach in ordinary classwork which eliminates successfully this serious drawback.

Orff-Schulwerk

The avoidance of written notes allows for swift progress in the early stages, but a dependence upon repetition, cliché and improvisation can bring its own bottleneck. The approaches used in much Orff-Schulwerk resemble the aural approaches used in language teaching which have been shown to be unsatisfactory when used in total isolation. Without the underpinning of literate understanding, there is an illusory element in the progress. Sooner or later, the teacher and his class have to go back to the beginning. For similar reasons, Orff-Schulwerk on its own seems to contain the seeds of future difficulties.

Pop and rock

One of the main differences between this work and Orff-Schulwerk lies in the less predictable nature of pop idioms. Even though a Blues sequence is, in a sense, a musical cliché, the children using it become involved in chords and chordal relationships. This in turn must lead to some sort of literacy even if it is merely a letter C representing the chord of C major. An understanding of this provides an intellectual seed from which may grow a form of literacy which is appropriate to the work being done. Here again, however, the reading and writing skills are not readily applicable to other kinds of work.

Classroom orchestra

As with the percussion band, classroom orchestra is dependent upon literacy, though here, pitch is being taught alongside rhythm. If it is well structured, the reading lends depth to the work. It does not serve as a barrier to progress.

Timbre

Again, principles are not involved. There is nothing intrinsically 'better' about the sound of one group over another. The comments below are brief and subjective but worth considering before embarking on any single scheme.

Percussion band

The range of sounds is limited but not without possibilities. In the traditional percussion band, the contrasts obtained from wood or metal sounds, struck or shaken sounds, loud or soft sounds, are often subtle and attractive. Similarly, in the avant-garde area, the variety obtainable exceeds expectations. Nevertheless, the continuing absence of sounds of definite pitch does lead to a musical craving which can become uncomfortable.

Recorders

The most unvaried of all the activities under consideration. Long stretches of descant recorder playing can be exhausting for the ear. Partwork offers some alleviation.

Orff-Schulwerk

Similar to percussion band in some ways, Orff-Schulwerk offers variety of timbre within a restricted zone. The mode of attack on pitched percussion produces a uniformity of sound which diminishes some of the advantages found in using instruments of varied construction. The sound is dry and is not helped by the repetitious nature of the work.

Pop and rock

This could become wedded to the sounds of the guitar and drumkit, but there is no necessity for it to do so. There is plenty of room for instrumental variety while still retaining something of the essence of pop and rock idioms.

Classroom orchestra

Here we have at one and the same time the greatest and least variety in timbre. The comprehensive score offers an attractive blend of sounds not found elsewhere in classroom activities. However, the early stages of the work demand that all instruments play together in the same rhythm and this produces a corresponding uniformity of overall sound. It can be varied by changing percussion instruments during the course of a piece, by using smaller forces for repeated sections and other strategies.

Idiom

Percussion band

Traditional percussion-band work could be in any idiom. It is, after all, merely an exercise in fitting percussive sounds to an existing piece of music. The music could be written by anyone from Lully to Lennon, but most published material derives from the corpus of 'classical' music. A more up-to-date selection might help to revive the activity. The Self/Dennis approach is rigid in idiom – indeed the idiom is a large part, too large a part perhaps, of its *raison d'être*. There is value certainly in introducing children to a wider vocabulary of sounds, especially when they are producing the sounds themselves, but if the work occupies all of the lesson time, the 'old sounds in class' might be forgotten. The concentration of attention on to idiom above all else seems to indicate an attempt to raise a comparatively small aspect of music to a pinnacle of importance which is hard to justify.

Recorders

Here, there need be no assumptions about idiom. The work is inclined to be of a traditional nature, but suitable modern material could be used to advantage. Bonsor's compositions like *Beguine* and *Hoe-down* work very well with selective groups. More elementary arrangements in the same mould would serve as welcome additions to the repertoire for classwork.

Orff-Schulwerk

The Method is the idiom. Orff-Schulwerk might remind us a little of medieval music, the gamelan music of Indonesia, Stravinsky, or, most of all, Orff's own compositions, but in general it is very much itself, both in idiom and in timbre. Unlike pop music, Orff-Schulwerk triggers off no automatic cultural associations. Its idiom grows out of its procedures.

Pop and rock

All the books and articles on this branch of music education focus on the idiom. How else can the work be defined? If it strays too far from its Afro-American origins, it becomes something else. If work in this idiom is to occupy the whole of the music curriculum, the children's musical education will become impoverished because there is so much worthwhile work to be done in other styles. However, few people have suggested that pop-orientated activities should occupy such a dominant position.

Bearing in mind that this kind of work must serve as part of the syllabus only, there can be no objection to idiom, as opposed to other considerations, being thrust so forcefully into the limelight.

Classroom orchestra

Class in Concert is in a fairly traditional style. Functional harmony plays an important part as do well-worn rhythmic patterns. However, there are no fixed boundaries. A teacher might construct his own scheme in any idiom from ersatz-medieval to that of the Second Viennese School. It is important for children to have the satisfaction of playing 'right' notes and it is for this reason that some of my music is fairly predictable. The importance of musical experience is paramount. A slight loss of adventurousness in the end-product justifies the process which is a heightened quality of musical participation.

Method and Methods

Methods tell us what to do. Presumably Kodály, Orff, Suzuki and others thought that they knew best: that they had the definitive answers to certain problems. Remarkably few British teachers of music have adopted Methods wholesale. 'A bit here and a bit there' seems to be the prevailing practice and should therefore serve as the starting point for development.

However, method (rather than *a* Method) must enhance a course of work. We can structure learning and experience by structuring materials and teaching approaches. This is not exclusiveness: it is simply efficiency and wisdom working hand in hand.

Lesson plans

The two lesson plans below relate to Orff-Schulwerk and classroom orchestra work respectively. Both lessons would take place early on in the courses.

Lesson Plan 1

Objective: By the end of the lesson the children will have developed some instrumental techniques and listening skills.

Enabling Objective: By the end of the lesson the children will be able to improvise answering phrases on tuned percussion instruments and will be able to distinguish between three notes of different pitch.

Equipment: Tuned percussion instruments stripped of all bars apart from E and G with A available alongside. A bass xylophone with the C and G bars in place.

Introduction: Revise previous work through rhythmic drills with body sounds, transferring to 'question and answer' work on pitched percussion, using the notes G and E over a bass xylophone ostinato of C and G.

Development: Place the A bars on each instrument and introduce its sound. Point out that it is higher in pitch than G.

Holding a glockenspiel so that the class can see it, introduce an imitative question and answer session (not improvised) within a two-bar (4/4) framework.

Continue, but with the instrument on the table so that imitation is aurally rather than visually based.

Set up an ostinato of minims using C and G on the bass xylophone plus half the class playing: . The other half of the

class take it in turns to improvise a short phrase within the framework: two bars ostinato; two bars ostinato plus improvisation. Continue until each child has improvised once. Exchange the rôles within the class and repeat the exercise.

Conclusion: Split the class into groups to devise their own ostinati and improvisations using the notes E, G and A only.

Lesson Plan 2

Objective: By the end of the lesson the children will have increased their musical literacy and instrumental techniques.

Enabling Objective: By the end of the lesson the children will have understood the symbol for and the meaning of a crotchet rest. They will have grasped the concept of 'staccato' and will be able to play in a staccato manner.

Equipment: Classroom instruments and orchestral instruments for those who play them. Music, which appears on pages 62, 63. (The remainder of the lesson plan appears on page 64.)

Hesitations by William Salaman

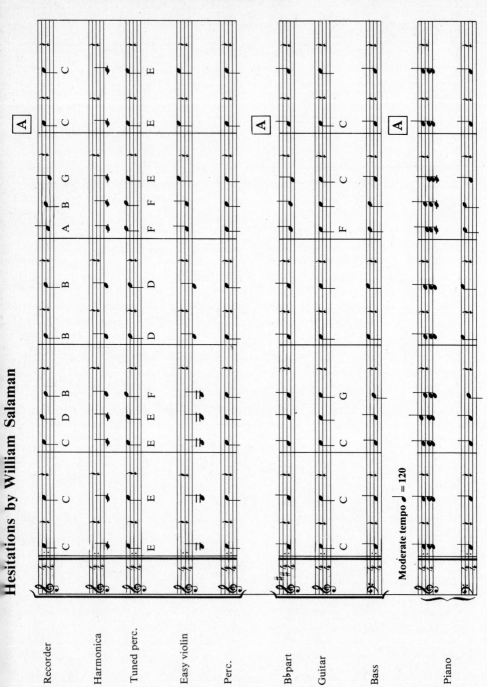

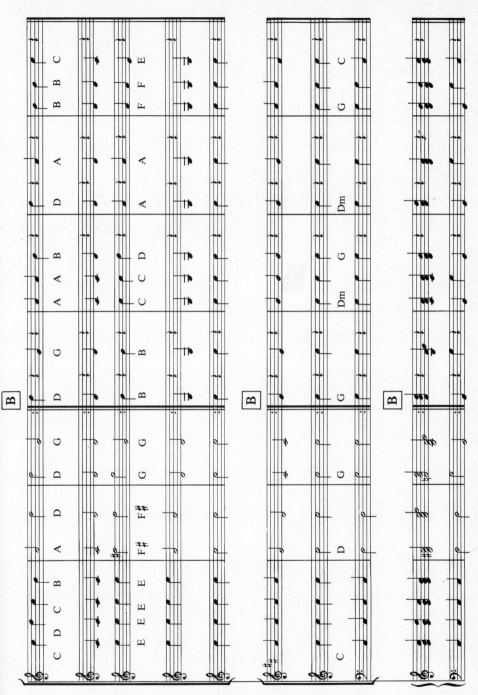

Introduction: Play 'Hesitations' on the piano (No. 4 in *Class in Concert*, Grade A) with the children following their parts. Explain the crotchet rest. Point out that some notes are played in a detached manner. Explain the word 'staccato'.

Development: Rehearse the music part by part and then together in accordance with usual rehearsal procedures. Draw attention to the crotchet rests and their purpose.

Write an exercise on the blackboard using numerous crotchet rests and invite individuals and then the whole class to clap it through.

Return to 'Hesitations' and work at the staccato style until the playing is satisfactory.

Conclusion: Play and record 'Hesitations'. Play back the recording and discuss the performance with a view to finding areas for improvement.

6 INVENTIVE MUSIC-MAKING IN THE CLASSROOM

Well within living memory, the standard treatment for a scald was to smear butter on the injured part. Quite suddenly, it was made known to both the medical profession and the public that not only was the new remedy to be cold water, but that the worst possible expedient in these circumstances was to apply any sort of grease to the burn. Very soon, it was accepted that white was black and this curious little volte-face has been generally forgotten. However, it has been replaced by others. Various kinds of food, modes of exercise and patterns of behaviour are the anathema of today, having been the cure-all of yesterday.

Education has had its share of somersaults. In the teaching of language, literacy and numeracy, the pendulum has swung with astonishing violence at times. The rules of grammar are vital one day, irrelevant the next. One generation can chant its multiplication tables while another can explain what 'base 6' means, though the two generations may find little common ground for discussion. At the centre of this volatility exists a bewildered teacher who has woken up one morning to find that he has taught the wrong material in the wrong way since he entered the profession.

The techniques and subject matter of teaching must change. Inevitably, some of the changes will be dramatic and correspondingly painful for teachers. In music education, such a wrench has been rare, largely because new ideas have been presented as additions rather than alternatives to the regular diet. However, some of the advocacy for creative music-making has been offered as a challenge to teachers. When I first encountered the ideas, I received a firm impression that I had to take it or leave it. There could be no dabbling. I was slow to understand what was being demanded of me. Swirling impressions of unconnected strictures and exhortations filled my mind. It seemed that moral values were being attached to many aspects of music education, that groupwork, avant-garde procedures, invention, the integration of the arts and self-expression were 'good' while more traditional concerns such as notation, tonality, metre, method, singing and information about music were 'bad'.

I became confused and resistant but at the same time I was aware of a nagging twinge of curiosity. I started to read books. Certain passages confused me further:

Today all sounds belong to a continuous field of possibilities lying *within the comprehensive dominion of music*. Behold the new orchestra; the sonic universe! And the

65

new musicians; anyone and anything that sounds. (M. Schafer, *The New Soundscape*, 1969, p. 2)

As far as I could understand, this had little to do with music or music education. Many authors seemed to see something I could not. I found it hard to believe that I could be so blind and insensitive. However, on reading John Paynter's books and articles I started to regret having placed notions of creative music-making on the lunatic fringe. Here was someone offering new approaches supported by rational argument and practical suggestions but without the moral tone that characterised the writings of so many others.

Paynter's ideas are manifold but two seem to be of overriding importance: inventive processes and groupwork.

Inventive processes

Of course I was aware that children could compose, but the suggestion that they could compose as a class intrigued me. My first reaction to the idea was sceptical: 'Fundamental to composition' I thought 'is technique and musical literacy, and in any case, the noise of thirty composers will be unacceptable. I shall not consider it further.' But I did consider it further. I asked myself what the creative process was. Maybe the singing and playing we did was creative. After all, there is a significant difference between a drab, inaccurate performance and a lively, precise one. Do we not 'create' the better performance? The answer to this is that we do indeed create the performance but we do not create the music. The music is still the composer's and what creativity we show is being put to his service. This argument seemed watertight to me but a little too cerebral. I needed the confirmation of my feelings and this was readily forthcoming. Having composed music myself, I knew exactly what a 'creative feeling' was like. Just as people are born and bred, so is music. The music I wrote was 'born' at the time of its composition. I was its parent! The music we prepared in class was being 'bred'. I was now its foster-parent!

So the work we did was not really creative, it was re-creative and as such did not seem to accord with Paynter's ideas.

Paynter has laid heavy emphasis upon 'decision-making':

> It is one thing to know what sounds are available and even to have experienced them. It is another thing to use them to create music. The essence of this lies in selecting the sounds we need (and/or which we are able to control) and rejecting those which do not fit our purposes. Exactly the same basic decisions would apply to creative work with any materials. Educationally the need to make decisions about these matters is of value and here music can play as important a rôle as any other creative activity.
>
> (*Music in Education*, 31 (1967), 662–6)

I found this view reiterated in other of Paynter's writings and formed the impression that he regarded this aspect of musical work as a fundamental principle for all music education. It worried me. I could hardly claim that the 'traditional' activities which took place in my music room involved significant decision-making. They fulfilled my principles, but not Paynter's. If decision-making were to be held as a principle, the legitimate activities within the music curriculum would be narrowed down to one corner of musical experience. I rejected the idea, regarding it as being irrelevant to my work. Suddenly, I realised Paynter was not offering decision-making as a principle for the whole of music education, but as a concise guide for *creative* work. If the children are making real decisions about their handling of sounds, then they are, by definition, creating music. It was later on that I worked out what a 'real' decision was. At that time my notion of musical decision-making was hazy indeed.

Having established that creative work could form part of my work, that I did not have to be 'born again', I could hardly deny that processes of this sort would be valuable. I knew of the satisfaction of composition and I could see that similar experiences could be of benefit to my pupils if only I could find ways of organising the work.

Paynter has drawn parallels between music education and education in the other arts. Just as an art lesson offers children a chance to experiment and create, using the materials of an artist – paints, clay or egg cartons – so a music lesson should offer the 'raw materials of sound' for a musically equivalent purpose. Most of the children I taught possessed a modicum of musical literacy, but I could see that it would not be of much service to them as the 'raw materials' for creative work. I could have taught them to construct eight-bar melodies with an answering phrase and the last note on the tonic, but rather than set their imaginations free, it would have acted as an exercise in constriction: a sterile, quasi-mathematical test. I needed a framework which could be understood by the children and within which they could invent with some freedom.

I chose Orff-Schulwerk, but my approach was a little different from that described in chapter 5. Every class had had experience of classroom orchestra, so it seemed unnecessary to return to the beginnings of musical experience. In an attempt at combining the benefits of classroom orchestra work and Orff-Schulwerk, I devised a scheme whereby I retained my usual 'score' of classroom and orchestral instruments, but wrote music which alternated tutti passages with episodes suited to improvisatory work. The improvisation was confined to individual recorder and tuned percussion players and also to those orchestral instrumentalists who were present. The others (harmonicas, guitars etc) provided a discreet chordal accompaniment. The activity was successful with the more able children, but the less able failed to grasp the framework within which they were supposed to improvise. Often, the results were haphazard. Many of the children made it clear that they preferred the anonymity of the re-creative work to this newly imposed obligation to make public utterance. Some seemed to have little to utter.

I blamed myself for this. The conception had been unsuitable. The group was too large and the improvisatory tasks had been too taxing. But, at the same time, I began to question the notion that this style of improvisation was creative in the broader sense of the word. The most successful improvisations came from children who had acquired the firmest grasp of the formula for improvisation. They were not selecting sounds or making decisions so much as discovering the notes which fitted into the prevailing harmonic and rhythmic framework. In one sense, the more successful they were, the less creative they were being. The fact that there could be several possible 'right answers' did not alleviate the doubt.

Before continuing this account, I must return to the other important feature of creative music-making, namely, groupwork.

Groupwork

The wife of a music teacher I know once confided to me that her husband would wake up regularly at about four o'clock in the morning, screaming threats and insults at the unruly mob which was destroying his music lesson. So vivid was his nightmare, he lashed out in all directions while she sought refuge behind a pillow. The curious feature of this story is that he never had discipline problems with his classes in real life. Still, most of us feel at times that our authority is supported by a certain measure of bluff – that calm and purposeful though our lessons *appear* to be, the nightmare is not all that far away. This element of defensiveness in our attitude can suggest to us that central control in the classroom, albeit of a benign nature, is vital. The corollary to this is that groupwork could be tantamount to professional suicide.

To those who have used groupwork, such a train of thought is absurd. Experience has shown that disorder does not arise when groupwork is properly organised. To those who have not used groupwork, a few commonplace observations might help in reducing fears of nightmares, the essence of which is confrontation: 'the mob versus me'. If I teach these thirty children properly, they will co-operate, they will behave as professional pupils should. We shall work together towards a commonly shared goal. But suppose I do not teach them properly? Thirty people against me is enough to reduce my chances of survival to nothing. However, if I split them into groups, their cohesion is destroyed. It will do no damage to their work because I will contemplate such organisation only when the activity is more productively pursued through group work anyway. It will make concerted misbehaviour almost impossible. In a phrase: 'Divide and rule.'

When I took my first plunge into groupwork, I felt that I might be opening a door to scenes of chaos matched only by the pictures of Hieronymus Bosch. I was delighted to find that nothing of the sort occurred. Misbehaviour was not a problem. This is not to suggest that my lesson was free from problems. Among the groups was one which was avoiding the tasks I had set. I found the children sprawled about a practice room chatting about the events of the day. Two members of the group were quietly doing some homework. I was distressed by this lack of interest and assumed that the blame for it could be laid at the feet of the very notion of groupwork. However, as similar situations arose, I became philosophical. There are always a few children who are barely interested in a subject. My subject could be no exception. The fact that they were displaying their lack of interest in a group as opposed to displaying the same lack of interest sitting at desks was hardly significant. As a matter of course, I would do what I could to spur the group into working. The results were generally drab, but there was no riot – no nightmare.

The purpose of groupwork in music lessons is not primarily managerial. Rather, it lies in setting up the best conditions for inventive work to flourish. As in some drama lessons where children within groups bounce ideas from one to another in order to create a dramatic miniature, so in music, they can decide between themselves the best approaches, and, of course, fewer players can be formed into a useful 'chamber group' capable of producing a varied end result.

I was struck by the opportunities offered in groupwork. Using classroom orchestra material, I sent some groups away to sort out their tasks in nearby practice rooms while two or three groups worked in the main music classroom. I did not pretend that this work was particularly creative. I was borrowing an idea from Paynter and using it for re-creative activity. Many of the groups produced polished chamber versions of classroom orchestra pieces. This mode of working served as a useful variation on our usual 'full orchestral' lessons, but the latter remained the norm. I was grateful for the new impetus given to the work in the classroom but the philosophy (as opposed to the methods) of inventive music-making worried me still.

The avant-garde

Everything seemed to point in one direction. The kind of work which best suited unskilled invention was the same as that which best suited groupwork: the avant-garde. Or, to be more precise, sounds which resembled the avant-garde, especially that of the 1960s.

Much of avant-garde music is intensely complicated. For most of us it is more difficult to imagine, write down or re-create music in this idiom than in more conventional idioms. We must assume that avant-garde composers know what they are doing, that they can hear their compositions with the inner ear. Children cannot possibly do this. The nearest they can get to it is through the production of pastiche avant-garde.

There is no simple way of defining the avant-garde in music, but, like the product of Orff-Schulwerk, it is recognised instantly for what it is. Broadly speaking, one might regard the more recent avant-garde composers as being those who have placed emphasis on matters of colour, texture and density and who have eschewed the more traditional preoccupations with melody, harmony and metre. Ways of arriving at the sound are threefold:

1 *Predeterminism* – of which the serial techniques are best known. The composer's choice of notes is severely circumscribed. In educational music, the

notes might be determined by the throw of dice or a game of snakes and ladders. (See Self, *Make a New Sound.*)

2 *Anarchy* – in which connections between sounds and other considerations are severed. An example is found in *Imaginary Landscapes* by John Cage, where twelve radios are tuned into twelve different stations simultaneously. In music education, some suggestions for inventive work fall into this category, or approach it. When children are instructed to create music without being given musical or other criteria, the result can be anarchic. Such productions are impossible to assess because the children have not been given specific goals to aim for. At best, they might be judged on the 'quality of creation', in other words, on the process, regardless of the product.

3 *Musical judgement* – all composers choose the sounds they use or else they consciously surrender their choice either in favour of some predetermined formula or to chance. We cannot expect children to understand the implications of musical predeterminism or anarchy. They might compose along these lines, but, in doing so, they are thrusting into the background the essential acts of making musical decisions, of selecting and rejecting sounds. If they are to make genuine choices, they must exercise musical judgement, and this also is a highly sophisticated exercise, especially when the sounds resemble the products of avant-garde composers: in other words, when the familiar comforts of traditional harmony and metre have been eschewed. It is up to any composer to convince his audience that he has exercised his musical judgement well. Though the sounds may be startlingly unusual, they must speak to us and be free from obscurity. We might feel that the music of Messiaen and Berio communicates with us immediately whereas we may find a measure of obscurity in some works of Birtwistle and Carter. Though our reactions will tell us more about ourselves than about the composers or their music, the issue of obscurity in music will be highlighted. Musical judgement must be made within a musical context. Professional composers convey the context within which their judgements operate. The clearer the context, the less obscure the music appears. Unless children are working within contexts which they and their audience understand, their products will almost certainly convey elements of obscurity and raise doubts in the minds of listeners.

With regard to the uses of avant-garde procedures and sounds in education, I found predeterminism, anarchy and obscurity equally unacceptable. Because of this, I could not bring myself to initiate a course of pseudo avant-garde work in my school. Yet I felt still that, given well understood boundaries, inventive procedures could open up new areas of opportunity for both my pupils and myself.

The need for decision-making

In the classroom, I had pursued improvisatory work with a little success and had used groupwork with some encouraging results, but I felt that I was dabbling. At the same time, I became aware of a tussle going on inside me. I had been musically trained in a formal academic mould. I needed notation and other traditional props for my musical good health. I could not bring myself to believe in the worth of formulae-based improvisations, though I could see no other way of taking advantage of the benefits of groupwork which, rather late in my career, I had come to value.

It seems useful for children to make decisions, and in an arts subject, the making of artistic decisions must be of special importance. But what is an artistic decision? The construction of a largely predetermined piece of music does not involve much decision-making. In anarchic music, 'anything goes', so the decision can be irrational and irrelevant. In music which is obscure, decisions are made indeed, but the nature of the result raises a further question: what decisions are worth taking? If a decision to select one sound rather than another is based on thoughts such as 'I like it' or (as some knowing children might think) 'Sir might like it', it indicates a poor educational background in music.

Decisions must be made with rigour, not necessarily intellectual rigour, but as a result of musical thought and sensitivity which has been properly nurtured in a methodical manner. Some suggestions for creative work encourage such rigour through limiting the task to obtainable specifics: explore the possibilities of one kind of instrument; relate your invention to one particular literary or pictorial stimulus. By these means, children and teachers can form judgements about the decisions being made. Because the task is defined, predeterminism, anarchy and obscurity can find little, if any, foothold.

Inventive work in class involves processes which encourage children to become increasingly aware of sounds and their potential for imaginative use. I had launched a course of musical education in my school which was somewhat unrelated to those processes. I taught singing and instrumental playing, and we listened to music a good deal. My vehicle for increasing the musical experiences and achievements of my pupils was notation, though I must emphasise that it was always a means to an end. I felt that decision-making and inventive processes in music were important, but I needed to relate them to my other work in class.

The account of my solution to this problem is offered neither as a revelation nor as an alternative to other people's conclusions. It tells of what I, an academic musician, had to do in order to make myself comfortable in my mind while, at the time, offering the children a chance to invent and make decisions within the realm of music.

Notation as a basis for inventive work

The classroom orchestra occupied us a good deal. The children learned the pieces with appropriate diligence and pretty soon each class had a corpus of titles under its belt. I have mentioned that I sent the children away to work at 'chamber' versions of the music. These miniatures were delicate facsimiles of the full orchestral sound and as such they were pleasing. I was thrilled to hear my own compositions treated seriously and carefully by the children. It was when I was rescoring 'O Little Town of Bethlehem' for the school orchestra to play at a carol concert that I was struck by my own arrogance. A certain self-satisfaction had settled upon me as I altered this harmony and inserted that cadential fanfare. I became aware of the level of 'double-think' to which I had stooped. Here was I, enjoying making inventive decisions around 'O Little Town of Bethlehem', while at the same time I had been insisting on faithful realisations of my own music from the children. Why should they not exercise their judgements on my music? My text was not sacred. They knew the music well and could surely devise some imaginative variations on what they knew.

Excited by this idea, I duplicated the scores of the music and divided the classes into large groups – three groups of ten – and sent them away to invent some variations on the familiar music. The results were deeply disappointing. Indeed, there were few results. The children did not know where to begin. I passed from group to group, suggesting cymbal clashes here and staccato tonguing there, but I had to admit failure. It didn't work.

As I had done before, I sat down with pen and paper in order to organise my thoughts:

The children must make valid decisions about musical sounds.
They will do this best with music they already know.
They will benefit through working in groups.
How can I devise a framework for this decision-making?

The last of these thoughts caused me to discern the root of the problem. I had given the children too much latitude and too little in the way of a framework. I must confine the activity so that they can understand what they are attempting to achieve. In short, I had abandoned the principle of structured teaching. With the pen still poised, I made a list of the categories of musical variation that could be tackled. Realising that the children would find the freedom I offered them strange in the first instance, I listed as their first task something small and specific (in all cases, I explained the technical terms with care):

'Play the music through a number of times with different dynamics. Play it soft, play it loud, or play it somewhere in between. At times, only two or three people need play. Try to organise the music so that a shape or form emerges. Don't forget the possibilities of crescendos and diminuendos.'

Next, I chose tempo:

'Play the music through a number of times, sometimes slowly and sometimes fast. Think what alterations are needed in order to get your own part to fit in convincingly. You may have to repeat notes on instruments which fade, like the glockenspiel. Don't forget the possibilities of accelerando and ritenuto.'

Finally, I chose instrumentation:

'Play the music through a number of times, each time changing the "colour" of the sound. Can you play the recorder part on tuned percussion and vice versa? How can the unpitched percussion instruments be used to bring extra character and variety to the music?'

Back at school, I divided a class into their groups and presented them with the specific tasks. This time, the work was purposeful, and, though the results were a little lacklustre, there seemed to be enough impetus for us to try again. We did. Gradually, groups improved. They tackled different pieces from the three viewpoints and each time, it seemed, the results revealed an increasing sense of form and musical awareness.

The children were making simple but important decisions about dynamics, tempo, instrumentation and form. Well aware that more than this was possible, I set out some new tasks – tasks which could be tackled successfully only when the more elementary work had been accomplished.

Of these new tasks, the first revolved around rhythm:

'Play the music through a number of times, varying the notation where necessary in order to create sections of different but definite character. For example: a march followed by a minuet, followed by a rumba, followed by a waltz.'

This task required some advanced skills and it was only after I had given the group considerable help that they were able to 'distort' the note lengths rather than simply apply dynamics, tempo variations etc. It was worth the effort, because through the attempt, the children began to analyse the real nature of a rumba or a waltz and at the same time they were making quite sophisticated inventive decisions.

The second task was directed towards ornamentation of melody and accompaniment:

'Play the music through a number of times, adding extra notes (or leaving some out) where it seems appropriate to do so. Look at the possibilities of passing notes, trills, repetitions and so on.'

The third task allowed for greater latitude of invention:

'Find new ways of harmonising the melody. The main melodic line must be present, even if the note lengths are changed. However, you need not use any of the other printed parts. The melody may be played on any instrument, or passed from one instrument to another. For accompanying sounds, think about using chord clusters on the piano, your voices etc.'

The last task suited the slower music better than it did the fast.

A few practical problems arose out of these activities. Some of the performances were anaemic through the absence of a piano. Occasionally, an adequate pianist was present in the group. Sometimes I played the piano myself, trying to do it in a manner which accorded with the group's wishes. Generally, there was no pianist. Curiously, we became accustomed to the sound (characterised chiefly by a lack of bass) and the shortcomings did not appear to inhibit progress or enthusiasm. Another drawback was the use of scores. Though I had duplicated copies for each group, I had to insist that they did not write down their ideas on the scores themselves, since the copies would be used by other groups later on. The pupils used separate pieces of paper for recording their thoughts and they also relied upon their memories.

The work described above was based on my own classroom orchestra material. I was simply applying the old adage: 'proceed from the known to the unknown'. The children I taught knew these pieces, so the same music provided the obvious starting point. Other starting points in the realm of traditionally notated music can be found in *Group Music Making* by McMurtary (Longman, 1972), in the Middle Eight Music Kits or even in a familiar song. Further ideas might arise out of an Orff-Schulwerk composition, but, best of all, a teacher's own material can form the basis of invention provided he is prepared to 'let go', to allow the children to do what they will with it, within an established framework.

Creativity and course structure

Though the results of this kind of work emerge as modest and generally unsuited to public display, they are important as discernible stepping stones between re-creative and creative work. Whether the sounds are 'new' or 'old', their roots should be apparent and the decisions which were made in their conception will have been based on rigour − not whim. This is not to suggest that other approaches are not equally rigorous. Teachers whose syllabuses are inventively based throughout will find different routes to results which have meaning and rigour. Inventive work is not an easy option within music education. At times, it has been offered as a cure-all, a recipe for instant success. I am convinced that this view is dangerous and can be damaging. Peril awaits those who swap horses in mid-stream, or, to pursue the analogy, those who try to ride two horses at once without first harnessing them together.

Creativity in the inventive sense is one of three facets of musical experience, the others being performance and listening. Its comparatively recent emergence as a force in music education has been supported by a wealth of literature. A baby needs plenty of care and attention, so it seems fair that this new arrival should be well nurtured. The books listed in the appendix include schemes for inventive work with tape recorders, synthesisers, *objets trouvés*, voices and instruments. Some authors have shown a healthy awareness of classroom realities. Others have not. Sifting through the choices of activity takes patience and determination. I have found that the three principles described in chapter 2 apply as thoroughly here as elsewhere.

According to the first principle we must ask whether the work is suited to the majority of children. Much of musical exploration is, especially when matters of instrumental skill and musical literacy are relegated to the background. Some avant-garde sounds and techniques (serialism in particular) are less accessible, however.

Is the work active and participatory? Almost by definition, work of this nature must be active, but if predeterminatory and/or anarchic procedures are used, the essential action of skilled decision-making may be by-passed. If the making of artistic decisions is to serve as a principle for creative work in particular, then the essential and central activity must be the making of those decisions. The absence of genuine decision-making suggests the absence of 'activity' in this context.

Is the work structured? It is here that we have to be especially careful. A creative project must have an assured educational basis. We must be sure that the children have been changed as a result of the activity, and we must be able to measure or discern that change. An inventive free-for-all will throw up random results because of its random inception. A project that requires inventive processes within clearly understood boundaries can be judged properly and built upon. But it is not only the individual projects that need structure – the whole pattern of projects needs an equal measure of organisation. The work might be compared to the growth of the individual. We pass from nappies to toddlerhood. We attend school and develop skills. Some of us move on to higher education and most of us develop partnerships and settle down in an occupation. The manner in which we, as individuals, react to these stages cannot be determined, but there is little question of the stages themselves being avoided. Similarly, a scheme of inventive music-making, like any other, is best devised as a logical process. The products of each stage cannot be foreseen, but a structured framework is necessary for fruitful musical and personal development.

One possible structure could be akin to that described in this chapter, where skilled activities based on musical literacy branch out into inventive work. Another might be built on a course of timbre education. Here, the children would explore in turn sounds derived from wood, metal, the voice and other sources. When each timbre is fully understood, work in which different timbres are used in combination will be invested with controlled understanding. Yet another might be linked with extra-musical stimuli: poems, pictures etc. This should begin with the most modest of challenges. A single word, such as 'insects', would offer sufficient *restriction* to focus imaginations on to a manageable corner of the available possibilities. As the selective skills develop, more ambitious enterprises such as the depiction of a haunted house or incidental sounds for a display of slides can be tackled without loss of meaning or direction.

Creative work in music suits integrated artistic activities well. Witkin, Ross, Small and others have advocated this development fiercely. Again, it is John Paynter who has put forward practical suggestions to make its realisation possible. Together with Elizabeth Paynter, he has produced *The Dance and the Drum* (Universal, 1974) which offers enormous scope but at the same time defines the limits. Few of our schools have set up integrated arts departments or faculties. Often, problems of architecture and timetabling prevent such work from getting off the ground. Added to this, many secondary school teachers, particularly teachers of music, display a general unwillingness to integrate. Until conditions and attitudes change, integrated artistic activities are unlikely to play a large part in the school curriculum.

Lesson plans

The two lesson plans below are concerned with the early stages of inventive work within different spheres. The first involves the children in explorations of sound while the second opens up the link between creative and re-creative work.

Lesson Plan 1
Objective: By the end of the lesson the children will have advanced their creative skills through the exploration of instrumental and vocal timbres.
Enabling Objective: By the end of the lesson, the children, working in groups, will have constructed small pieces in ternary form, using instruments of similar substance or voices.
Equipment: Musical instruments as available.
Introduction: Demonstrate and explain the differences between wooden sounds, metal sounds, the sounds of the piano and the voice. Suggest different ways of exploiting one kind of instrument. Briefly explain ternary form (A B A).
Development: Split the class into groups of five, instructing each group to devise a piece in ternary form using wooden instruments, metal instruments, the piano or voices. Move among the pupils, offering help.
Conclusion: Perform pieces. Record. Play back and discuss.
Note: This lesson might be more effective if all the groups were to work with the same timbre. Such a suggestion presupposes an unusual abundance of instruments.

Lesson Plan 2
Objective: By the end of the lesson, the children will have begun to explore the possibilities of varying printed notation.
Enabling Objective: By the end of the lesson, the children will have adapted a familiar piece of music working within the fields of dynamics, tempo or instrumentation.
Equipment: Classroom instruments and duplicated scores of a classroom orchestra arrangement of 'Lightly Row'. (The melody will be found in Priestley and Fowler, *School Recorder Book 1*, p. 17.)
Introduction: Play the arrangement as a classroom orchestra. It has been learned in a previous lesson, so needs no rehearsal. Suggest different dynamics and play it through at varying speeds.
Development: Divide the class into three groups of ten children. One group will work at the piece with a view to creating effective dynamic contrasts. Another

will work on varied tempi, possibly resulting in a gradual accelerando. The third group will experiment with different instrumentations. All groups will be asked to repeat the piece as often as they consider necessary in order to allow time for all their variants to be effective.

Conclusion: Perform the three versions. Record. Play back and discuss.

A German Folk Tune

7 LISTENING ACTIVITIES IN THE CLASSROOM

While classes of children struggled to pitch high Es with their voices, to manipulate their recorders or to understand dotted crotchets, I was consoling myself with pleasant thoughts of the listening lessons which were yet to come. Like the hazelnut cluster in a box of chocolates, it was being saved to the end as a delayed pleasure. How many evenings had been spent in tracking down or writing music which could be singable or playable by the children? How many lessons had been spent in sorting out notation, fingering and interpretation? None of this would be necessary in the listening lesson. The whole field of musical literature from plain-song to pop was waiting to be revealed – a treasure chest. All I had to do was to lift the lid.

The memory of my interview came back to me:

'How are you going to cope with the difficult children in the classroom?'

'I shall make music *interesting* for them.'

'And how are you going to do that?'

'All music is interesting, isn't it? There's so much of it. I shall share my enthusiasm with the children.'

As the first listening lesson drew near, I began to realise that this wealth of interesting music was something of a problem – an *embarras de richesse*. I would have to classify the music into areas of interest and deal with each area in turn. I sorted out some broad categories.

'Great' music. Beethoven, Brahms and the others. I loved being a dwarf among these giants. They lifted me up and swept me away to a different plane of experience. Of all music, this must be the most important. The experience must be shared. The great tradition must be passed on.

The avant-garde. This is the music of today. Like modern life, it can be harsh and difficult to understand, but must be faced. Through gaining an understanding of such music, my pupils might also gain the ability to sort out other thorny encounters.

Medieval music. A delightfully fresh and naive sound, belonging to our tradition, yet much neglected. As an educator, I should help to nurture a better-informed generation of listeners. At the same time, the music has an immediate appeal which allows for easy presentation.

Pop music. Much of pop music contains original thought and expressive power. It can justly be claimed that this music belongs to the young. They understand it and love it. I would be foolhardy not to capitalise upon such a basic advantage. As disc jockey, I shall choose only the best examples and the children will learn how to listen rather than just hear in an area where their natural enthusiasm lies.

Pleased with this scheme, I thought I would start in a dramatic manner, using Beethoven's Symphony no. 5 to stun my class into silent awe. For me, the music was important. It constituted my first experience of classical music. I had been told all about the connections between the opening motif, Morse code, Churchill's victory sign and the war. In my boyhood, it was broadcast on the radio almost every week and, as a professional musician, I had played it several times with intense involvement. Such powerful music, I thought, cannot fail to captivate its listeners. I shall say nothing – the music will say it all.

The class waited in open-minded silence. The disc rotated. The stylus descended upon the groove:

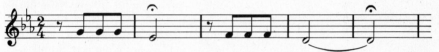

To my astonishment, the children started to titter. A few fierce looks quelled this irreverent reaction and the symphony pursued its course against a sea of apparently blank ears. I found my own attitude towards the music changing. My response was no longer one of spiritual uplift. An uncomfortable defensiveness began to grip my being. My mental fist was banging an imaginary table: 'This is *good*', I protested inwardly, 'I *know* it's great – it's part of *me* – it's part of *everyone*.' Amid these anguished thoughts, I recalled the interview. 'I shall share my enthusiasm with the children.' Well, I could be neither more enthusiastic nor more willing to share, but something had gone awry.

At the end of the first movement (I had never guessed that I would be grateful for its brevity) I asked the children what they thought of the music. 'T's'all right, s'pose', was the general reaction. I told them about Churchill and the war. A certain languor descended upon the class. With appalling swiftness, I realised that 'the war' was over. Maybe I was keeping it alive out of deference to my parents' generation. For the children it was a strange, distant event about which teachers seemed to enjoy reminiscing.

Neither the music nor its associations appeared to touch these children. I went home very depressed that evening, but pretty soon some comforting thoughts arose from the ashes of the lesson. How could I be sure that Beethoven's masterpiece had been a damp squib for everybody? Maybe that hearing had kindled a few flames which would shine brightly later on. And what had I expected anyway? Enthusiasm about music of this sort has little, if any, overt expression. We do not normally show our appreciation by grimacing in ecstasy and I could hardly have expected anyone to shout 'Bravo!' after the last chord. Perhaps there *had* been a response. Perhaps that titter was an involuntary reaction to an unexpected *frisson* induced by the opening notes. On the other hand, perhaps not.

Other classes reacted in a similar way to the Beethoven symphony and to the other great works that I offered such as the *Academic Festival Overture* by Brahms and the Piano Concerto in B flat minor by Tchaikowsky.

I hoped for a more lively involvement in the avant-garde selection. I realised that I was entering a difficult area, so compromised before starting by reclassifying the music as 'modern'. I chose pieces that might have entered the children's subconscious through television and elsewhere. I played records of Stravinsky's *The Rite of Spring*, the opening of *Also sprach Zarathustra* by Strauss and parts of the *Háry János* suite by Kodály. The colourful orchestration of these pieces should capture the children's attention like a three-dimensional film. Indeed, the children did respond when they recognised television theme tunes, but, with that excitement over, they lapsed into apparent uninterest.

I thought I had reached the lowest point in pupil reaction with medieval music, but, as it turned out, that exquisitely painful moment was reserved for pop music. I admit that my knowledge of pop was small and my enthusiam smaller still, but, out of a sense of duty, I sought advice from an *aficionado*, listened to the music in advance and devised a course of listening to pop music which would trace its more recent history through generally lesser-known but well-polished examples of the genre. The children were nonplussed. Pop music was something to chat to and to move to: 'If Sir says we can't talk and we can't dance, we won't do anything. And what is Sir doing with pop music anyway? Is he trying to be with it perhaps? How pathetic!' Their discomfort was my discomfort. I abandoned the course without hesitation.

Different strategies

This string of failures set me wondering. I had not lost my own faith in the music that I chose to present, but I had to accept that some invisible barrier stood between it and the children.

A free period. The music room was empty. I sat at my desk, thinking, staring at the aluminium window frames, the composition ceiling tiles, the breeze-block walls with their asbestos linings. 'There it is!' Beethoven and aluminium; Kodály and composition ceiling tiles; Machaut and breeze blocks; the Beatles and asbestos. We are mixing our rituals. School is a compound of rituals wedded by time to the architectural commonplaces that were greeting my eye. Academic striving seems appropriate in these bleak surroundings, while in contrast, Beethoven speaks most eloquently within the rituals of a concert: the hush, the tuning up, the tickets, the programmes, the black suits. I had been mistaken in trying to present concert music divorced from its attendant trappings. I was reminded of an occasion when my headmaster instructed form teachers to hold 'mini assemblies' in their form rooms with those classes that could not be accommodated within the hall. An acute sense of unreality attached itself to these sessions. Moral homilies and the muttering of the Lord's Prayer amid school bags strewn over the floor, notices about fire drill, and desks decorated with graffiti were inappropriate. The rituals would not mix.

It was not only the unsympathetic ambience of the classroom which militated against my listening lessons. The fact of using recorded, as opposed to live, music widened the distance between Beethoven and the children's sensibilities. We rarely question the prevailing view that a 'good' recording closely approximates to the original. Perhaps we should. A recording tells us as much about a live performance as a photograph does about a piece of sculpture. We have learned that the shading in the photograph implies curves and spatial relationships but at the same time we admit to an illusion. We cannot feel the sculpture or experience directly its ability to express the character of both the material and the sculptor. Similarly, the vibrant, tightrope-walking quality of live music is reduced in a recording. We are making do with a representation only.

Though I admitted the shortcomings of recordings, I knew that they would have to play a leading part in my listening lessons. I decided reluctantly that listening might have a purpose in school quite different from the rôle I had given it up to now. The children trek from French to maths to physics. They need relaxed refreshment. Perhaps my task is to offer some relief from the grind of school learning. I resolved to forget about 'greatness' and to forgo my educational earnestness. I would make my listening lessons a haven of peace in the hectic lives of my pupils. I would play records of music which made few, if any, demands on their minds or emotions.

I prepared programmes of lighter music. The overture to *Orpheus in the Underworld* by Offenbach, the *Karelia Suite* by Sibelius and *Rhapsody in Blue* by Gershwin were among my first choices. Many of the children seemed to enjoy these offerings. My more tolerant attitude towards a certain amount of chatting over the music provided an atmosphere free from tension. Quite soon, the children grasped that this was an 'easy lesson' and made suggestions for its improvement. Could they bring in their own records? I decided to adhere to my decision that this activity was intended, above all else, for purposes of relaxation, so could not refuse. From this there grew up a curious bargain – a sort of package deal: 'I'll tolerate twenty minutes of your music if you will tolerate twenty minutes of mine.'

It needed only a few weeks of this arrangement to convince me that I had really reached the nadir in my music teaching career. The lessons served no purpose whatsoever. The 'relaxation' was undirected and devoid of educational function. The children were unchanged by the lessons. There was no objective, no advance, no discernible experience. I was disgusted with myself for having allowed such a situation to develop.

This rejection offered no clues to alternative strategies, so I decided to list the areas of failure in the hope that something new would present itself.

Failures
  'Great' music
  Modern music
  Medieval music
  Pop music
  Music for relaxation
  Package deals

The earlier experiments collapsed because I thought (wrongly) that the music would attract the children like iron filings to a magnet. The later experiment collapsed because I had not foreseen that 'relaxation' was such an empty, spineless concept. I began to wonder whether I should direct the music towards the children, not the children towards the music. Deeper appreciation of the masterworks is dependent to some extent upon background knowledge and previous musical experience. My pupils did not have these so they lacked the equipment with which to understand the force of the music which I offered them. How could I overcome this problem? There is music which sweeps *any* listener away through sheer force of character. Examples are *Et Exspecto Resurrectionem Mortuorum* by Messiaen, *Eight Songs for a Mad King* by Maxwell Davies and parts of *Billy the Kid* by Copland. All of these use shock tactics. The bells in the Messiaen, the musical symbolism of a deranged mind in the Maxwell Davies and the gunfight in the Copland are highly unusual strokes of genius that could not fail to enter the consciousnesses of the children. In a sense, the music would do the work. It would come to them.

They were a little intrigued by these pieces and their attention was held for a time, but the response was very much less intense than I had expected. I found this hard to understand until, one weekend, I took a three-year-old nephew to London Zoo. Our conversation went like this:

'Those are flamingoes. They can stand on one leg for hours.'
'Can I have an ice-cream?'
'Look at that ant-eater. His nose is all pointed so he can reach the ants in the ant-hill.'
'I want a ride on an elephant.'
'Shall we look at some snakes which are longer than your bedroom?'
'You said I could have an ice-cream.'
'That ostrich can run faster than I can drive our Mini. It's the biggest bird in the *whole world.*'
'Look! There's a man selling ice-creams.'
We ended up eating ice-creams on the back of an elephant.

My nephew had taught me an important lesson. We cannot marvel at the unusual until we know what is usual. His apparent inability to recognise the unique qualities of the animals bore a similarity to the inability of my class to share my excitement over the unique qualities of the music. The distinctive features of the music by Messiaen, Maxwell Davies and Copland were, to my classes, only 'slightly' unique. Their awareness was sufficient for them to sense that these works were not everyday musical occurrences, but they absorbed them rapidly into their general experience of musical sounds. If they had possessed a much closer acquaintance with the niceties of musical classification, they would have appreciated the special qualities of these dramatic pieces more readily. A philatelist is excited by a misprinted stamp. To those of us who are not philatelists, it is just another stamp.

I was beginning to despair of finding many other ways of approaching listening to music. One, of course, was well known to me – programme music – music that tells a story. I had avoided this source of material because of a long-felt unease about the use of music for literal communication. Very rarely indeed has music evoked precise images in my mind. Even when I have been told in advance what the music is supposed to depict, I have been in doubt. I get lost in *The Sorcerer's Apprentice* of Dukas. I can see little of Shakespeare's Falstaff in Elgar's *Falstaff* while *The Hebrides* overture by Mendelssohn reminds me no more of Fingal's Cave than it does of other places in the British Isles. Precise imitations of nature have seemed to me almost embarrassingly commonplace on account of their realism. Examples are the asses braying in Saint-Säens's *Carnival of Animals*, the sheep bleating in Strauss' *Don Quixote* and Delius' famous cuckoo.

If I was going to introduce programmatic music to my classes, I would choose that which evoked moods rather than that which told stories. As a start, I selected *Prélude à l'après-midi d'un Faune* by Debussy, *Pacific 231* by Honegger and the *Sea Interludes* from *Peter Grimes* by Britten.

Of all the approaches tried so far, this was the most successful. The children latched on to the programme easily and seemed to enjoy the stimulus to listening. I added to the works for listening *Mars, the Bringer of War* from *The Planets* suite by Holst, parts of *Sinfonia Antartica* by Vaughan Williams and some movements from *Pictures at an Exhibition* by Mussorgsky. Despite the children's pleasure in this music (they often asked to hear pieces again), I was dissatisfied with the apparent lack of cohesion which should have been present in a course of work. I asked myself whether this kind of listening programme met the principles I had decided upon as yardsticks for measuring the worth of activities in class. Was it suited to the majority? It seemed that it was. Was it an active participatory pursuit? I thought that the children were participating in the sense that their attention and imagination were occupied with the sounds that they heard. Was the work structured? No! There was no progression. Only one of the goals of experience and achievement was being met. The children were experiencing examples of programmatic music, but their achievement was undefinable, probably non-existent. The listening needed purposeful order and I could think of none to give it. However, one important fact of music-teaching had emerged. The ear needs help. This help could be a musical programme. What else might it be?

Score reading

The answer lay in activities which we had already been pursuing. Before learning a song or an instrumental piece from notation, the class generally followed the notes on the stave while I played them at the piano or sang them. Up to now I had not regarded this as 'listening'. I thought of it as a routine procedure before moving on to the more difficult tasks of making music as a class. Obviously, it is easier to follow than to sing or play and I left it at that. I now felt it was time to look at this aspect of musical perception more closely.

Kodály, Orff, Suzuki and others have pointed out that the growth of language in children follows a well-defined sequence. First, the baby imitates and begins to build a vocabulary. Then he constructs his own word orders and uses them for more complex communication. After that, generally at school, he learns to read. Finally, he learns to write. There is no special reason for musical growth to pursue a similar path, but Kodály and the others have argued that it should and their Methods of music education are based upon this theory. For one of the crucial stages in musical literacy there is little in the way of a parallel in the development of language literacy. This is the skill of following music as it is being performed. I think of it as 'half-reading'. We recognise the written signs as symbolic of the sounds we hear, but we have no obligation to translate them into sounds ourselves. A great deal of skill is needed to hear inwardly the exact pitch and rhythm of even one line of music, but to 'half-read' the same line is straightforward enough.

The fact that it is easy is not the reason for including it among classroom activities. The main strength lies in its offering a means for the eye to assist the ear with the consequence that the children become much more involved in what they hear. It is easily susceptible to structured teaching and focuses attention away from the seemingly intractable problems of idiom and 'greatness'.

Noel Long advocated score reading as a classroom activity in *Music in English Education* (Faber & Faber, 1959) and he supported his beliefs by publishing a series of score-reading books, 'Listening to Music' (Boosey & Hawkes, 1963). Roger Fiske's series, 'Score Reading', reveals a greater awareness of the problems of musically illiterate beginners, but, even here, the pace is too rapid for assured success. Other series have used graphic symbols to help the children to follow the shape rather than the details of the music.

One of the first difficulties I encountered was that of the meaninglessness of the notes and other symbols to the children. When following a single stave, some were confused by bar lines. They thought they represented notes. In Fiske's series, the first complete item is the well-known Minuet in G by Bach. It uses few time values: crotchets, quavers, minims, dotted minims and crotchet rests. The melodic line is characterised by wide leaps in some places and smoothness in others. Once pointed out, these features provide 'landmarks' for the children. I found it best to play the right hand part alone in the first instance. Having reached the end of the first line I moved to the second, only to discover that some of the children had become confused. They thought the left-hand stave constituted the second line to be followed. I had not foreseen the possibility of this error and it reminded me again of how slowly and carefully I should proceed. I needed to know how well my classes were managing with the problems of score reading, so I devised a simple scheme for tracking down exact notes. This was particularly useful for music without bar numbers or rehearsal letters. I numbered the lines of music (or 'systems' as they are correctly called), then the bars within the system and finally the notes within the bar. A common procedure might consist of my playing a piece on the piano and stopping suddenly: 'Where have I got to? Hands up.' An answer might be: 'Four, seven, two' meaning: 'Fourth system, seventh bar, second note.' I had no qualms about stopping and starting, talking while the music was playing or extracting a few notes for special repetition. I was teaching; the children were learning. Always, at the end of the lesson, I played the piece through uninterrupted and the children could follow it on the page with confidence. I learned a few useful techniques as the lessons went by. When playing the music for the first time, I would call out as much useful information as I could: 'Next system starts now! ... Follow the left hand part for two bars ... Watch out for the upward leap of the melody', and so on. Piano music was especially well suited to this work so I duplicated copies of easy pieces, by Schumann in particular, in order to build up confidence in following two staves. Book 1 of Fiske's series (*Orchestration*) moves through increasingly complex scores in a fairly logical manner. It needs only a few supplementary items to make the pace of learning realistic.

When I introduced recorded music, I was able to check the children's understanding more easily because I was no longer wedded to the piano. I instructed them to follow their scores with the blunt end of a pencil. As the recording played, I moved between the chairs on the look-out for pupils who needed help. Their fingers or pencils quickly told me this. The most common cause of confusion was tied notes. To see two notes and to expect to hear one appears illogical on first acquaintance. I used cassette recordings for ease of starting and stopping.

As the work progressed, I was able to draw the attention of the class towards instrumental colour, form, dynamics and so on. This kind of active listening suits the conditions of a classroom. For me, it reopened the doors which had seemed to be closing all around me. Because my efforts with Beethoven, Stravinsky, Machaut, pop, the avant-garde, 'shock tactics' and programme music had ended in some degree of failure, I had mistakenly concluded that none of these kinds of music could be suitable for listening lessons. Now that the activity was properly structured and offered scope for real achievement, the idiom and classification of the music receded in importance. The experience of following the score of a Schubert song is similar to that of following the score of a Lennon song, but, with the scores removed, a cultural bogy enters the arena and achievement is much reduced.

Listening worksheets

Some of my confidence had been restored. I knew for certain that children could listen to music in a specific manner. I considered other areas which might offer an equal boost to their attention. Once again, I realised that there was potential in what we had already been doing. Just as playing through melodic lines in singing and instrumental lessons had triggered off thoughts of score reading, so playing back to the class recordings of their own work initiated a more organised kind of listening activity. As a matter of course, I had recorded classes and groups when they had brought their work up to performance level. The playing of these recordings often led to suggestions for improvement and general discussion. I decided that these recordings could be analysed more closely. Having listened to the recordings with care, I prepared worksheets. In the case of a classroom orchestra piece, the worksheet might read as follows:

1 In what way do the percussion instruments make the music sound more lively?
2 The title of this piece is 'Waltz'. From this recording decide what are the main features of a waltz.
3 The music is marked 'allegro' which describes the speed. What do you think it means?
4 Suggest two ways in which more variety might be obtained.
5 Listen to your own playing in the recording. Does it seem to be too loud, too quiet or about right?

The children found this activity absorbing. When they were performing, the concentration upon their own musical responsibilities prevented many of them from being much aware of what was going on around them. The recording was an ear-opener and the worksheets helped to direct their attention towards it in specific ways. This kind of work is not new. It has been used for many years in C.S.E. examinations, but with younger, non-specialist children there is little motivation to analyse unknown music performed by unknown musicians. The use of their own work provided the right kind of incentive for concentrated listening and for tackling the worksheets enthusiastically.

With groupwork, the procedure was a little different. Only a few children had been involved in the music's creation, so, apart from being present at the recording session itself, the others were hearing it for the first time. I set questions on the worksheet which could be commented upon verbally by the performers after the others had written their thoughts on paper. Here is an example:

1 List all the instruments used in this piece.
2 Name three ways in which the tambourine was played.
3 The music is in three sections. How is contrast between the sections obtained?
4 Two instruments were used in unconventional ways. What were the instruments and how were they played?   •
5 Suggest one way in which the piece might be made more effective.

I asked a number of children in the class to read out the answers they had given to the questions. The performers acted as authorities and at times demonstrated some of the techniques they had used. We then moved on to a recording of the work of another group and a new worksheet.

This kind of listening lesson is time consuming. I set aside entire lessons and found that the ability of the children to listen critically increased quickly. Though listening of this kind is not overtly structured, it is bound to follow the logic of the work which is being listened to. I presented questions on the worksheets which related the children's listening skills to the other concepts which were being learned and absorbed.

Associated listening

With listening now established as part of the music curriculum, I was tempted to re-introduce it without relating it so closely to the children's own performance, or to score reading. An idea of integrating a number of musical activities within one lesson has been favoured by Keith Swanwick. I felt that this offered a reasoned approach which I should try out. The underlying purpose is to link varying musical experiences to a common theme. This should not be confused with well-established 'project' work in which a theme such as 'the sea' forms a focus for several activities. Rather, a *musical* idea such as the rhythm 𝄞 ♩ ♫ | ♩ ♩ | might be common to all the experiences, and each can lend deeper meaning to the others.

The rhythm quoted above is central to the second movement of Beethoven's Symphony no. 7. It features also in the song 'I've been to Harlem'. A lesson might consist of the learning of the song, some echo-clapping based on the rhythm and some listening to the symphony without scores, though the notation of the two-bar rhythmic phrase could be written on the blackboard. From this varied diet, the children will have increased their vocal repertoire, they will have learned a little notation, and they will have listened to some music with focused attention.

I taught some lessons along these lines, but two difficulties arose which forced me to abandon the approach. Firstly, the planning of such lessons took too long. To find well-matched activities was a laborious task. Even when I found some material for listening and singing or playing which linked up felicitously, often one or other piece would contain some distracting feature which would have been impossible to 'explain away' to the children. The second problem was more fundamental. This kind of lesson planning fights with notions of long-term structured learning. The song might suit the 'theme' of the lesson, but it might fit badly with my scheme of vocal education. Similarly, the choice of music for listening suited only the 'theme'. It belonged to no continuum of listening which is essential for a convincing and cohesive music course.

Though this kind of integration was too demanding for me, I found it most helpful in triggering off ideas in similar vein. Almost every playing and singing activity suggests related listening. If the children play a waltz, they will increase their understanding of the style by listening to one (and dancing one?). Songs with a national flavour suggest that other music from the same country is suitable for listening. If a composition by some of the children is exploiting a clearly discerned timbre or texture, then an appropriate composition by a professional composer can only illuminate their efforts more clearly. Suggestions of this sort appear in many books but, once again, most eloquently in Paynter's writing. His book *Hear and Now* (Universal, 1972) is closely concerned with these connections in music teaching, but is weighted heavily in favour of contemporary music. These excursions into relation listening are illustrative only and I have found that two or three minutes of recorded music to 'make a point' is plenty.

Conclusion

The ordeals of the listening lessons were the hardest of any within my classroom experience and maybe, as a result, I learned most from them. I might have learned more quickly if I had paid closer attention to lesson planning and the threads of reason that underlie it. I had worked out that the main aim of my entire music course was that the children should gain worthwhile musical experiences and a sense of achievement. I had formed some broad objectives, which, if met, would fulfil this aim. These objectives covered the areas of performance, invention and listening, supported by the learning of notation, vocal technique and instrumental skills. I had decided that each lesson would have an enabling objective. This would be precise and measureable or discernible. All this made good sense to me. I could know whether the enabling objective had been met or not. If it had, some of the objective would have been met and in turn I could be certain that bit by bit I was achieving the main aim of the course. As my early listening lessons were disintegrating, I regarded educational theory as the last quarter I would visit for help. What is the point of a lesson plan if the children fail to respond to the work? Why frame an objective about what the children will do if they simply will not do it?

I realise now that my problems lay in the fact that I did *not* frame objectives about what the children would do. I might have phrased the objectives in those words, but, in essence, I was giving *myself* objectives. '*I* will play them a record of Beethoven's Symphony no. 5 ... *I* will introduce them to some modern music.' Seen as objectives for *me*, they were easy to measure or discern. Yes, I did play them a record of Beethoven's Symphony no. 5! I was hoping that the children would be overwhelmed by the greatness of this music. That would have been a rather strange objective: 'By the end of the lesson the children will have been overwhelmed by the greatness of Beethoven's Symphony no. 5.' And even if that had been the objective, how would I measure it? Seen from this point of view, it is hardly surprising that so many of the listening activities failed. I should have had more faith in the reliability of small enabling objectives, each one measurable or discernible. In score reading, an enabling objective might read: 'By the end of the lesson the children will be able to follow a string quartet score. They will have begun to acquaint themselves with the alto clef.' In a lesson which is built around worksheets and recordings of the children's work, an enabling objective might read: 'By the end of the lesson the children will have begun to analyse how variety is obtained in the context of a classroom orchestra piece. They will be able to spot errors in performance and should be able to offer suggestions for improvement.'

These objectives are realistic. They can be met and I can *confirm* that they have been met by asking questions, by obtaining written answers or through skilled observation.

The ears are merely doorways into people. Certain forms of experience are gained through the ears, but the ears themselves do not need educating. All they do is hear. I think I was trying to educate the ears of my pupils during many of those listening lessons. I was impressing them with Beethoven, I was bringing them up to date with Kodály, I was soothing them with Offenbach, I was shocking them with Messiaen and diverting them with Debussy. The heads and the feelings which lay between the ears were largely untouched until I succeeded in finding a connection between what the ears heard and genuine involvement and achievement.

Lesson plans

Of the lesson plans below, the first relates to score reading while the second relates to the children's inventive work around a classroom orchestra piece.

Lesson Plan 1

Objective: By the end of the lesson the children will have extended their score reading skills and will have developed their knowledge and understanding of musical form.

Enabling Objective: By the end of the lesson the children will have followed a score in four parts and will understand minuet and trio form.

Equipment: Copies of the third movement of Mozart's Serenade in G, K.525 *Eine Kleine Nachtmusik*. Cassette tape recording of the same. Recording of Mozart's Symphony no. 29 in A, K.201.

Introduction: Having distributed the scores, explain the layout and play the piece through calling out bar numbers, pointing our repeats etc. as the music progresses.

Development: Play the first violin part on the piano up to the first double bar. Explain that 'tr' = 'trill'. Play a trill. Draw attention to the octaves between the first and second violin parts in the second section and to the rests in the other parts. Play the recording, drawing attention to the repeats. Explain that this is the minuet and that the trio follows the same formal pattern. Play the recording of the trio, stopping frequently to ask individuals for bearings (e.g. fourth system, second bar, first note). Point out the texture of this trio – a melody with

(continued on page 92)

Eine Kleine Nachtmusik - Third Movement

Menuetto

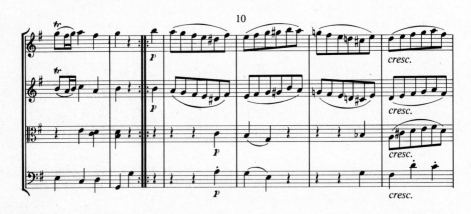

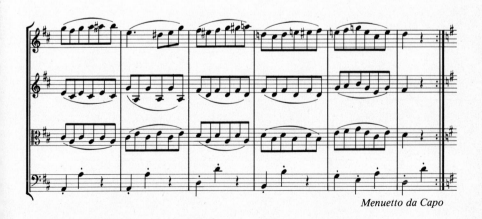

Menuetto da Capo

a light bass, the inner parts providing harmonic figuration. Explain '*Da capo*'. Play through the entire movement, passing among the pupils to give help where necessary.

Conclusion: Play the minuet and trio from Symphony no. 29 pointing out the similarity in form.

Lesson Plan 2

Objective: By the end of the lesson the children will have developed their ability to listen analytically.

Enabling Objective: By the end of the lesson the children will be able to discern variations in timbre and texture.

Equipment: A recording of an ensemble piece made by a group of children from another class using notated scores but with their own variants added. Scores and parts of the music, classroom instruments and worksheets.

Introduction: Distribute the instruments and music. Play through the piece as a classroom orchestra. Distribute worksheets.

Development: Play the recording five times, instructing the class to answer one question on the worksheet after each hearing.

WORKSHEET

1 What dynamics are used in this performance and where? $f = forte$ (loud); $p = piano$ (quiet); $mf = mezzoforte$ (in between).

2 At one point the recorder and tuned percussion players swap parts. In which bar does this begin to happen?

3 How do the players make the ending of the music sound triumphant?

4 Describe two ways in which the players achieve changes in volume.

5 When the main section is repeated, the trumpet makes a different sound. What has the player done second time around?

Ask around the class for individual answers and listen to the recording again.

Conclusion: Discuss the inventive features used by the class who made the recording and suggest how they might be used by this class in a future lesson.

8 LIVING SCHOOL MUSIC

I have discussed a host of opportunities for music teaching. Indeed, to the undecided, a somewhat warlike host it may appear. We can imagine a battalion of soldiers advancing like pawns towards us. On the breastplate of each is inscribed a different legend: Kodály; Curwen; National Heritage; Vocal Creativity; Orff; Percussion Band; Recorders; Classroom Orchestra; Pop and Rock; Invention; Score Reading; Worksheets; Supportive Listening. Behind the soldiers trundles a baggage train, the wagons labelled: Literacy; History; Form; Skills; Idiom. Which soldier will I allow to capture me? Which wagon shall I use for my supplies?

For each of us the answer will be different, but the ways of arriving at our answers may be similar. We have to weigh two factors: what the children require for a balanced musical education; and what we, as teachers, are capable of offering. The first of these is straightforward enough. It is now widely held that all children should be given opportunities to create music, to perform music and to listen to music. Every music teacher should possess skills with which to nurture these three facets of musical development, but even with a firm intention of doing so, he might find himself at a loss as to how to bring any one of them about.

In the creative sphere, for instance, he might opt for improvisatory work within a Blues framework or work towards the handling of avant-garde textures and sounds. Maybe he would be better advised to encourage his classes to invent variations on notated music that they know already. All three possibilities are creative but is one of them best? It is here that the second factor – what the teacher is capable of offering – comes into play.

There is no ignominy in failing to possess every musical skill. We all have strengths and weaknesses and it would be altogether impracticable for a teacher to embark upon a programme of work in which he has little or no expertise because he has been swayed by a value-laden argument. Though there is an obligation to offer the children inventive opportunities, the decisions relating to idiom, method and the like should be reached in the light of one's skills and interests, not through any sense of moral association. I see only damage being done when value judgements are brought into decision-making of this kind. Yet it happens. We find arguments like : 'It is *better* to pursue avant-garde creative programmes because the avant-garde is the most significant development in today's music.' Or: 'It is *better* to pursue rock and pop creative programmes because these are the idioms

93

in which children can find natural expression.' Or: 'It is *better* to base creative work around notation because only notation can provide a secure foundation for musical understanding and development.' All three arguments fail to make the vital distinction between primary and supportive factors in music education. The avant-garde processes, the pop and rock idioms and musical literacy are merely supportive of the primary activity of creative music-making. Precisely the same arguments apply to the skills of performance or listening. School children should be given the chance to perform and to listen to music. Whether the performance is brought about through Orff-Schulwerk, recorder playing or any other medium is not a moral issue. Similarly, the way a teacher chooses to conduct listening lessons is his concern alone. Whatever the activity, its prime purpose is the creation of opportunities for living musical experience.

Musical experience is artistic experience. (The Mad Hatter and his friends might remind me that this is not the same thing as saying artistic experience is musical experience.) To embark upon a detailed discussion of the nature of artistic experience would exceed the scope of this book, but a general consideration is vital if justification for music as a school subject is to be found.

Several lines of argument for the retention and development of arts curricula in schools have been put forward. Of these, three in particular are heard quite often. The first is that today's children must be educated for leisure. With shorter working hours and high unemployment, the focus on spare time should be more intense than ever. That young people should occupy this time profitably must be a concern and responsibility of schools. The second is that the arts are useful. The skills and disciplines gained through arts activities can be adapted to the demands of commerce and industry, so, once again, schools must ensure that qualities of determination, co-operation, dexterity and so on are nurtured through arts education. The third is that the arts offer their own justification. 'Art for art's sake' encapsulates the view, suggesting a position of privilege in that such a self-justification renders the arts in schools immune from criticism.

The notion of education for leisure seems, at first glance, both sensible and easy to understand. After all, for most people, the hours of each weekday are divided fairly equally into work, leisure and sleep. However, closer investigation soon disturbs our assumptions about what work and leisure are. In Western society work is often regarded as a saleable commodity, sometimes unpleasant and burdensome, alongside which leisure hours lie empty, waiting to be filled. Despite this contrast, the activities which occupy working hours are scarcely distinguishable from those which occupy the leisure hours. A bricklayer might spend some of his spare hours playing the trombone in a local brass band while a professional trombonist could be building himself a garden wall. A motor mechanic might happily spend his evenings decorating his house while an interior decorator could be spending oily hours under his car with similar contentment. The cook is learning the piano while the pianist is cooking. And so it can go on. One person's work is another's play. Leisure cannot be described as absence of work or exertion. Some leisure occupations, such as patchwork quilting, demand enormous concentrations of labour. Others, such as motor-cycle scrambling, are dirty and dangerous while yet others, such as playing chess, ask for fierce mental concentration. Neither is leisure to be thought of as unpaid occupation, for if it were, it would have to embrace the activities of washing and ironing clothes, sweeping floors and sorting out income tax returns.

A mild questioning of the words 'work' and 'leisure' shows how much we assume about them, how loosely based our assumptions are, and how very difficult it would be to devise convincing courses in schools around concepts of education for leisure. In view of this, it is basically dangerous to categorise music principally as a leisure activity. To do so underrates music and, by implication, underrates the other arts as well.

Maybe the notion of usefulness in the arts will bear scrutiny more robustly. Even at the humble level of class music-making, children can learn to make independent decisions, to work together, and to develop special skills. Parallels are easily found in other arts subjects. Though these gains may indeed be adapted to the requirements of 'real' life, we are bound to ask in what way non-artistic pursuits are more 'real' than artistic pursuits and why it is that the extra 'reality', if it exists, is given such kudos by society.

Let us imagine that a school leaver has been selected from many applicants for a job in a microelectronics factory. His musical experiences in school have given him certain qualities sought after by the employers. It could be argued that music education has fulfilled its purpose simply through helping him to secure employment. However, it must be borne in mind that his dexterity, nurtured in music lessons, is being used in the assembly of calculators, and that whatever calculators assist, music assists also. The calculator lying in a drawer does nothing, but, put into the hands of an operator, it becomes most useful: much more useful than mere music. It saves time in shops and offices, and, with its big brother the computer, it is shaping a society in which the goals of efficiency and speed seem to be in sight. Speed and efficiency are the prized end-products which music has served in its very modest way. Dance, drama, visual art and creative writing can contribute in similar ways and with equal modesty. Provided teachers of arts subjects can adopt humble attitudes in the face of glittering speed and gleaming efficiency, they can justify their rôles in schools.

But, one day, these teachers might ask how they and everyone else are supposed to take advantage of the new order of things. They might wonder whether the main uses of the new gadgets should be to provide opportunities for pursuits which lie beyond the enjoyment of progress for its own sake. They might question the assumption that the arts have been useful after all, since the chain of usefulness appears to be turning into a circle of frustration, the links of which strain to pull each other along, only to find that they are pulling themselves, nothing changing.

I am suggesting that the profound qualities of the arts and artistic involvement cannot be put to the service of the mundane demands of material and physical existence and then be described convincingly as 'useful'. It must be the other way about. The stopping point in the hectic quest for change and progress must lie in the realms of artistic experience, not in the progress itself.

'Art for art's sake' is the third justification offered for the pursuit of arts curricula in schools. It is here that the most compelling arguments will be found, though I suggest that 'Art for our sakes' summarises the thesis more keenly. Active involvement in the arts must make us more acutely aware of ourselves. Our responses are real, important and immediate. We have no need to rationalise about future advantages or to harbour doubts as to how our work will benefit society. It is surely a quirk of present-day thinking that so high a value is placed upon production, comfort and leisure. We like to enjoy these advantages but most of us use them as a base from which to pursue less tangible but more real goals. These goals all lie within the realms of spiritual experience, not in the religious sense necessarily, but more in the sense of our active spirit: our *animus*. There is no necessity to ask *why* we spend so much time and energy on smearing oily substances on canvas, on reading stories which are not true, on drawing horsehair across strings, on watching people pretending to be other people on a stage. We *know* why. Psychologists and sociologists might dare to offer reasoned explanations, but explanations are not needed. We know. It is our glimpse beyond the daily round.

The intensity of feeling determines the level of our involvement. We may respond more readily to music than we do to paintings, or vice versa, but there is a common nature to both responses. Such artistic experience is as vital in education as it is in life and I suggest that it is *better* than experiences solely connected with progress or comfort.

Music can be 'useful': it can keep children off the streets, it can promote competitive spirit, it can serve as a gateway to fame even, but none of these benefits approaches its ability to provide immediate, living experience. Few ordinary children in ordinary schools will avail themselves of music in any specialised sense, so the long-term advantages will be lost to them. However, even with two lessons only each week during term times, they are able to achieve and experience at a modest level, which can provide them with a sense of fulfilment unmatched by golden predictions for the future.

It is not possible to extract the creativity from invention, the re-creativity from performance or the knowing response from listening any more than joy can be extracted from laughter or grief from weeping. So it must follow that we cannot teach 'creativity', 're-creativity' or 'listening responses' as though they were ordinary school disciplines. We can, however, nurture the conditions in which these experiences can develop and flourish. It is a task which demands toughness and sensitivity, patience and urgency, a firmness of purpose and an open mind.

APPENDIX: BOOKS AND MATERIALS

General introduction

The titles of books and materials in this appendix have been chosen for their relevance to the main body of this book. They are listed according to chapter, and, where necessary, divided further under subheadings. Where books on particular aspects of classroom work are included alongside related classroom materials, the books are listed first. In all cases, consideration of *structure* in music teaching has been a guiding factor. Materials which do not lend themselves readily to structured teaching have been omitted from the list. The comments which follow each title are intended to give readers an outline picture of the publication and an indication of its usefulness. Most of the books and materials are published in Britain. Some references are made to works which are out of print. Often, these materials are still sitting on classroom shelves and, in the case of books, libraries are able to acquire almost anything, given a little time. No magazine articles or songsheets are included in the list.

Given these provisos, the list cannot be comprehensive in any sense. It is a selection from the enormous output of music and books available to music teachers.

In order to keep abreast of new developments in music education, especially in the field of publications, readers are urged to consult *Music Teacher*, a monthly magazine published by Scholastic Publications (Magazines) Ltd, 10, Earlham Street, London WC2H 9LN and the *British Journal of Music Education* published three times a year by Cambridge University Press.

Other, quite recent, bibliographies have been prepared and these are listed below.

Bibliographies of books and materials in music education

Walkley, C., *Music Materials for the Primary School* (Schools Council Publications, 1976)

Consisting of five looseleaf volumes plus a supplement (1979), this comprehensive bibliography is available from the University of Reading Music Education Centre. The five titles are: 1. Song Material   2. Choral Works   3. Recorder and Ensemble Music   4. Teacher Material   5. Pupil Material. A great deal of the music listed is suited to lower secondary school classes. The compilation contains

97

a brief description of each publication. Mr Walkley confines himself to details of fact and does not offer any critique of the publications. This is probably the most thorough survey of its sort available.

Burnett, M. (ed.), *Music Education Review Vol. 1* (Chappell & Co., 1977). Burnett, M. and Lawrence, I. (eds.), *Music Education Review Vol. 2* (N.F.E.R., 1979)

Both volumes contain lengthy lists of materials for use in schools, though much of it is for extra-curricular work. Some contributors to the body of the books have appended lists of materials related to their special topics (e.g. early music). These selections might prove to be most helpful.

Farmer, P., *Music in the Comprehensive School* (Oxford University Press, 1979)

The 'Resources Appendix' to this volume contains brief opinions on books and on a few items of classroom material under headings such as: 'General Education', 'Philosophy of Music' and 'Sociology of Music'. The tone is generally positive throughout. The list will be particularly rewarding for teachers interested in pop music and its educational possibilities.

Chapter 2 Matters of principle

Rowntree, D., *Educational Technology in Curriculum Development* (Harper & Row, 1974)

There is little about educational hardware in this book, so the title is misleading. Rather, it explores the uses of objectives in short- and long-term lesson planning. The difficulties which most of us experience in this field are understood by the author and, though his message may appear to be a little divorced from classroom realities at times, it comes across with great clarity. The book should prove both stimulating and useful to teachers who are tussling with problems in course design.

Swanwick, K., *A Basis for Music Education* (N.F.E.R, 1979)

This is a serious book with some welcome flashes of humour here and there. It explores several fundamental issues in music education, at times illustrating points through the use of flow-charts and other favourite devices of educational writers. The chapter on 'The parameters of music education' is especially relevant and the discussion on the use of creative processes in class (chapter 5) offers a non-partisan view of the topic.

Chapter 3 Matters of fact

Marland, M., *The Craft of the Classroom* (Heinemann Educational, 1975)

The subtitle 'A Survival Guide' suggests a certain desperation which is not actually found in the text. The author has applied intelligence and commonsense to the problems which confront most classroom teachers. He does not delve deeply into the causes of disruptive behaviour or poor responses from pupils, but offers instead ways of dealing with such situations as they occur. Short though it is, the book is packed with wise observation and helpful advice.

Fontana, D., *Psychology for Teachers* (The British Psychological Society and the Macmillan Press, 1981)

This is a hefty book (though not expensive) covering every issue that its title implies. Dr Fontana's written style is easy to read and his organisation of subject matter allows one to dip without loss of understanding. Maybe the most useful section of the book is the last, 'Social Interaction and Teacher–Child Relations', which includes an illuminating chapter on class control and management. Whereas Marland (see above) offers immediate solutions to immediate problems, Fontana delves into the whys and wherefores of student *and* teacher behaviour. If a child is insolent in class, we will not rush to this book in order to learn what our reactions should be, but careful study of its contents during out-of-school hours will bring valuable awareness of the undercurrents which can govern the tenor of lessons.

Paynter, J., *Music in the Secondary School Curriculum – trends and developments in class music teaching* (Cambridge University Press, 1982)

In this book, Professor Paynter has devoted much thought and space to problems of classroom management. Indeed, this may be the first book by any author to discuss in depth the hurdles which must be surmounted by music teachers, as opposed to teachers of other subjects, working with groups and encouraging creativity. The bulk of the book is concerned with the more recent practices in music education, so that advice given quite properly relates to such matters as the encouragement of children to show musical initiatives and the organisation and supervision of several groups at once. The more humdrum topics like class singing and the routines for classroom orchestra are not explored in such detail.

Chapter 4 Vocal music in the classroom

Vocal technique

Hewitt, G., *How to Sing* (E.M.I., 1978)

There is plenty of useful advice here for the serious student. Indeed, the book is intended for performers rather than teachers. However, some of the techniques can be developed in class and, of course, if our own singing voices serve us inadequately in a lesson or a choir practice, any attempt to improve them should find assistance from this book.

Kelsey, F., 'Voice Training', in *Grove's Dictionary of Music and Musicians, Fifth Edition* (Macmillan, 1954)

This article is the length of a small book and covers many aspects of voice production which are relevant to classroom work. The basis of **bel canto** singing, which Kelsey examines in depth, can lie at the root of any voice-training where purity of sound is the main objective. The article does not appear in the sixth edition of *Grove's Dictionary, The New Grove.*

Rainbow, B., *Music in the Classroom* (Heinemann Educational, 1971)

This includes a chapter 'Teaching Singing' (not to be confused with 'Choral Music') which contains elementary advice about teaching singing to classes of children.

Newman, H. (compiler), *Fifty Canons and Rounds* (Universal)

Rounds provide an enjoyable and easy entrée to the skills of part-singing. This is a useful collection containing examples varying in degrees of difficulty.

Jenkins, D. and Visocchi, M., *Mix 'n' Match* and *More Mix 'n' Match* (Universal)

Correctly described as 'instant part-singing', these books contain quodlibets: tunes which can be sung together. Theoretically, the songs in a quodlibet should share a common harmonic foundation, but in some of these examples one's tolerance is stretched. Still, the collections offer opportunities for enjoyable and skilled music-making. Like rounds, quodlibets help to smooth the path into independent part-singing. In these books, up to five parts can be singing at once against an accompaniment of a single strand bass line or common chords on guitar.

The Kodály Method places heavy concentration upon both vocal techniques and musical literacy. The materials associated with the Method are listed under the next heading.

Singing and literacy

Musical literacy can be a strong foundation for singing, but there is an ever-present danger of singing becoming the means for learning notation instead. The Kodály Method uses sol-fa in a thorough-going manner in its early stages, the growth of literacy always serving the needs of musicianship. Most of the books and materials listed below relate to this Method.

Szönyi, E., *Kodály's Principles in Practice* (Corvina Press, 1973)

This short volume has an 'official' ring to it. It is packed with fact and explanation but offers no criticisms or suggestions for development of the Method. For teachers who decide to put all or most of their eggs into the Kodály basket, the book will provide a useful starting point.

Choksy, L., *The Kodály Method* (Prentice-Hall, 1974)

The Kodály Method is concerned largely with the adaptation of the Method to school conditions in the U.S.A. The kernel of the book, 'Kodály for American Schools', will be of interest mainly to teachers working in the U.S.A. However, there are over seventy pages of songs printed at the back of the book. These will be invaluable to anyone using the Method and should have an immediate appeal to older children. They serve the requirements of the Method at every stage.

Choksy, L., *The Kodály Context* (Prentice-Hall, 1981)

The Kodály Context examines the Method in a most penetrating manner. The book includes a section on the links between movement and the Method, and another section of special interest to secondary school teachers: 'Kodály for Older Students'. This section contains chapters on improvisation, listening and the application of Kodály principles in choral training. The book is easy to read and should serve the needs of the committed teacher very well indeed.

Vajda, C., *The Kodály Way to Music* (Boosey & Hawkes, 1974)

Kodály's Method has been thoroughly adapted by Vajda for use in British schools. She uses many British songs alongside those of other countries. The course is intended for the very young in the first instance, extending from singing games to more challenging activities. An emphasis upon the growth of musical literacy forms the backbone of the book which is generously supplied with music illustrations.

Swinburne, W.H., *The New Curwen Method* (The Curwen Institute, 1980, three vols.)

More than anyone else, Curwen established Tonic Sol-fa in Britain in the late nineteenth century. Similarly, the newer international interest in sol-fa can be attributed mainly to one person: Kodály. *The New Curwen Method* seems somewhat redundant in the light of Kodály's work, especially since, like Kodály, Dr Swinburne has abandoned several of Curwen's more archaic ideas. We have to search quite hard to find anything here whose presence adds extra significance to Kodály's thoughts. Still, its native origin will appeal to some and there are useful lists of song titles relating specifically to the learning of each new note of the sol-fa scale.

The Kodály Method is supported by a wealth of music written by Kodály himself. A brief survey is given below.

Kodály, Z., 'The Kodály Choral Method'. Edited by P. Young and G. Russell-Smith (Boosey & Hawkes)

50 Nursery Rhymes within a Range of Five Notes
These are original tunes by Kodály, clearly intended for the very young.

333 Elementary Exercises
These are very short and are designed to familiarise children with the pentatonic scale in its several inversions.

Let Us Sing Correctly – 107 Exercises in Two-part Singing
Intended for the practice of accurate intonation, the exercises are dry and hardly melodic. They would be of interest to those who are fully committed to the Method.

Bicinia Hungaria I–IV
These consist of 180 two-part songs with a few exercises interspersed. The early ones are quite difficult to perform and the later ones very difficult.

15 Two-part Exercises
These are similar to *Let Us Sing Correctly* but more advanced. They are often musically interesting. There are no words.
77 Two-part Exercises
66 Two-part Exercises
55 Two-part Exercises
44 Two-part Exercises
33 Two-part Exercises
22 Two-part Exercises
This material requires considerable vocal and reading skill. Towards the end of the series distant keys and highly complex rhythms are used.

Tricinia
This book contains twenty-nine advanced pieces for three voices (SSA or TBB). Many of them would sound well on instruments. There are no words.

Epigrams
These nine pieces are extended compositions for two voices or instruments with piano accompaniment. They are musically interesting and technically demanding.

24 Little Canons on the Black Keys
The first sixteen are notated in sol-fa only, the remainder being in staff notation. There are no words. They are, perhaps, more suited to instrumentalists than to singers.

Brocklehurst, B., *Pentatonic Song Book* and *Second Pentatonic Song Book* (Schott)
These are useful supports for the teaching of the Kodály Method, particularly when the work centres around pentatonic melodies. There are teacher's and pupils' books. The first Song Book contains songs of various nations mixed up somewhat randomly. The Second Book classifies the songs by nationality, Hungarian songs being absent! Chord indications appear in the pupils' books but sol-fa notation does not.

Singing and repertoire: pop music

There are many collections of pop music available, but few are realistically priced for schools and copyright laws inhibit teachers from pursuing simple solutions to the problem. However, the books listed below provide inexpensive, legally acceptable material for classroom use.

Attwood, T., *Pop Songbook* and *Pop Songbook 2* (Oxford University Press)
The two books contain forty-eight songs between them, with suggestions for their performance in many cases. Unlike most school songbooks, they come in one format only, there being no separate versions for teachers and pupils. Some of the songs have accompaniments written out on pages separate from the melody and words – a rather awkward arrangement. Others have no accompaniment so will require some 'busking' by the teacher or a pupil if piano is to be included. All the

songs are supplied with guitar chord indications and a few are provided with countermelodies for glockenspiels and other classroom instruments.

Singing and repertoire: folk

Leach, R. and Palmer, R. (eds.), *Folk Music in School* (Cambridge University Press, 1978)

Here is an essential book for any teacher who intends to work with folk music in depth. Many aspects of the genre are covered. Of particular interest are chapters 3 and 4 which discuss the uses of folk music in class. Chapter 8, 'Singing Style and Accompaniment', is also helpful. There is much else besides, including excursions into history, drama and English.

Palmer, R. (ed.), *Room for Company* (Cambridge University Press)

Like the other collections edited by Palmer (listed below), this one is both a history book and a song book. It deals with the history of sports, trades and social customs, the study of which should lend greater meaning to the songs. There is a piano part besides guitar chording. The melody alone is available also.

Palmer, R. (ed.), *The Valiant Sailor* (Cambridge University Press)

This looks at naval life between the years 1700 and 1900. The melodies have guitar chord indications but there are no piano accompaniments. This applies to the remaining Palmer collections.

Palmer, R. (ed.), *The Painful Plough* (Cambridge University Press)

The songs and information relate to rural and agricultural life in the nineteenth century.

Palmer, R. (ed.), *Poverty Knock* (Cambridge University Press)

Industrial songs feature here with some examples being a little more recent in composition than those in the other books.

Palmer, R. (ed.), *Strike the Bell* (Cambridge University Press)

All the songs in this collection are concerned with road, canal, rail or sea transport.

Palmer, R. and Raven, J., *The Rigs of the Fair* (Cambridge University Press)

The songs here evoke the grimy atmosphere of fairs and markets in nineteenth-century England.

Singing and repertoire: early music

Sargent, B., *Minstrels, Minstrels 2* and *Troubadours* (Cambridge University Press)

Minstrels is a most approachable collection of medieval music, the bulk of it being vocal. General suggestions for accompaniments are made in the introduction, but precise guidance for each song is not given. *Minstrels 2*, on the other hand, includes notated suggestions for repetitive rhythmic accompaniments and drones.

The music is a little more challenging than that in *Minstrels*. *Troubadours* is similar to *Minstrels*, much of the material being vocal.

Singing and recreation

There are many songbooks containing 'old favourites', but changes in fashion inexorably render them out of date after a decade or so. Bearing in mind that lesson objectives in this area relate to the memorising of socially useful songs, there is no special necessity for including notation in the children's books. The series of collections published by A. & C. Black, some of which are listed below, are splendidly up to date, and inexpensive pupils' books are available. These come in two versions, one with words only, the other with words and melody. The teacher's books include simple, imaginative piano accompaniments and chord indications for guitar, but beware; at times the two do not blend harmonically. They are alternatives. Descants for recorders and other instruments are provided for some songs.

Apusskidu (A. & C. Black)
Ta-ra-ra Boom-de-ay (A. & C. Black)

Between them, these books contain a multitude of attractive songs with no discernible cultural or national bias. They range from older folk songs to quite recent pop songs and also include some music hall numbers.

The Jolly Herring (A. & C. Black)

A mixture of folk and pop songs, the collection serves as a useful supplement to *Apusskidu* and *Ta-ra-ra Boom-de-ay*.

Mango Spice (A. & C. Black)

Forty-four Caribbean songs which are less well known and not always easy to perform make this a more specialised volume.

Harlequin (A. & C. Black)

This contains seasonal songs, some of which will be new to teachers.

Carol, Gaily Carol (A. & C. Black)

Many of these forty-three carols are refreshingly new. The well-known Victorian favourites are studiously avoided throughout, but more recently composed Christmas songs rub shoulders with attractive medieval material.

Vocal creativity

Schafer, M., *When Words Sing* (Universal, 1970)

There are exciting suggestions for imaginative vocal work here, few of them using traditional notation. Some of the projects could produce intriguing results, but anyone using them will need to be thoroughly convinced of the value of such work since the sounds are far from conventional. There are sixteen short chapters, each offering a distinct activity for voices, ending with exercises based upon the suggestions.

'Music for Young Players' (Universal)

This series has been given a misleading title since out of about sixty titles, eight are for voices alone and many of the others combine voices with instruments. Nearly all are graphically notated on single folded sheets of paper. A few come in pamphlet form. Composers in this series include George Self, Brian Dennis, John Paynter, Christopher Small, Bernard Rands and David Bedford. Most of the pieces are short and bear little or no resemblance to traditional vocal music for schools. Bernard Rands' *Sound Patterns 1* and *Sound Patterns 3* might be profitable starting points. Suggestions for the rehearsal and performance of pieces in this series will be found in Paynter's *Hear and Now*, pp. 59–67.

Paynter, J., 'All Kinds of Music' (Oxford University Press)

Book 1: Voices contains ideas for experimental work with voices. These will be found towards the end of the book.

Further material relating to creative vocal work will be found in the books listed under chapter 6 in this appendix.

Chapter 5 Instrumental music in the classroom

Percussion Band

Traditional Percussion Band

The popularity of pitched percussion work in schools has all but eclipsed the traditional percussion band which uses non-pitched instruments only. The band publications of Joseph Williams, Boosey & Hawkes, Cramer, Paxton, Novello, Curwen and others are now museum pieces. However, many schools still possess this music and the instruments to go with it. A revival of interest could be translated into practical reality quite easily. There is much that teachers can do in arranging pieces themselves. The book discussed below will be a reliable guide.

Adair, Y., *Music through the Percussion Band, Sixth Edition* (Boosey & Hawkes, 1966)

Now out of print, this book ran to six editions and can be obtained quite easily by libraries. In its way, it is as thorough as any Method within music education and the sixteen chapters cover the ground progressively and sensibly. At first, the work is aurally based. When the children are familiar with the instruments and have developed a sense of pulse, notation is introduced. There is advice on scoring, conducting, general management, working with older children, working with less able children and much more. Part 2 of the book describes musical games and exercises which will sharpen awareness and instrumental technique.

New Percussion Band

Here, the work is not confined to non-pitched percussion. Indeed, voices and body sounds are often recommended along with ordinary pitched instruments. However, much of the material can be, and often is, played solely on non-pitched instruments. The need for a precise interpretation of the graphic notation places this work more in the realm of the percussion band than in that of 'creative' music-making where, so often, inventive processes are encouraged.

Self, G., *New Sounds in Class* (Universal)

Described by its author as 'contemporary percussion music', this publication contains twenty-two graphically notated ensemble pieces. It is carefully structured and graded so that new symbols are introduced at a digestible pace. The introduction offers ample guidance for performance and each piece is supplied with suggestions for its preparation.

Dennis, B., *Experimental Music in Schools* (Oxford University Press)

This uses many of the techniques found in Self's *New Sounds in Class* (see above). Twenty pieces (called 'materials') explore similar arrangements of sound, using similar graphic notation. The teacher's book is well supplied with explanation and justification for the work and is designed to be used alongside the materials which are printed on separate sheets for class use. The latter half of the teacher's book discusses electronic music in the classroom.

Recorder playing

Dinn, F., *The Recorder in School* (Schott, 1965)

This slim volume starts from scratch and lays heavy emphasis upon some rather obvious realities of recorder work. Chapters 3, 4 and 5 should be useful to teachers working with recorders for the first time. In them, the author deals with matters of progression in recorder teaching and tackles some common problems such as varying abilities within a single group.

Simpson, K., *Music through the Recorder, 1, 2 and 3* (Nelson)

Of the many recorder tutors on the market, this is often regarded as being the best. One drawback is its comparatively high price, but, even so, there can be no better value in the field. Kenneth Simpson has set out to widen the musical benefits of recorder playing, hence the emphasis upon *music* in the title. He deals with matters of fingering and technique of course, but at the same time he uses recorder playing both as a means for understanding phrasing, form and harmony and as a basis for pupil composition. The work is well paced, easily understood and nicely presented. Priority is given to playing real melodies, but there are exercises provided to consolidate the skills as they are learned. There are teacher's notes in Books 1 and 2.

Salaman, W., *DuoKits 1–6* (Middle Eight Music)

All thirty-four duets are suited to recorder players ranging from near beginners to advanced executants. (See below under 'Classroom Orchestra'.)

Salaman, W., *Class in Concert* (Middle Eight Music)

These publications may be used as a basis for a course in recorder playing. (See below under 'Classroom Orchestra'.)

Winters, L., *Pleasure and Practice with the Recorder, Book 1* (E.J. Arnold)
This book contains a wealth of melodies for the left hand alone.

Orff-Schulwerk

Keetman, G., *Elementaria* (Schott, 1974)
Gunild Keetman collaborated with Orff for more than forty years, so this book must surely be regarded as an authoritative primer for Orff-Schulwerk. Despite its closely-packed 200 pages, it is described as 'a first acquaintance' with Orff-Schulwerk: an indication perhaps of the enormous body of thought and material that go to make up the Method. The book is thorough. Nothing is left to doubt. However, it must be said that the pace of explanation is unvaried and a certain determination is needed if everything is to be absorbed. The first half of the book covers instrumental work, touching upon singing only when it involves instrumental accompaniment. The second half concentrates upon movement training, especially with younger children. Anyone wishing to pursue Orff-Schulwerk in an authentic manner will find this book invaluable.

Hall, D., *Teacher's Manual* (Schott, 1960)
The reader is introduced to the basic concepts of Orff-Schulwerk from the viewpoint of instrumental playing. There is no mention of movement and very little of singing. The explanations are clear and concise. A teacher may feel confident to tackle rhythmic drills and simple improvisations over ostinati after reading this manual. Hall frequently refers to *Music for Children* (see below), copies of which should be at hand for reference.

Orff, C. and Keetman, G., *Music for Children, Vols. 1–5* (Schott)
Though possibly intended merely as examples of progress in Orff-Schulwerk, these volumes could serve as textbooks for playing. There is enough material to fill music lessons for years on end.
Volume 1 – Pentatonic
This contains: 1. Nursery rhymes and songs 2. Rhythmic and melodic exercises 3. Instrumental pieces, including rondos and canons. The music is realistically graded and painstakingly prepared. If the children are to play the pieces from notation, individual parts will have to be written out.
Volume 2 – Major: Drone Bass Triads
The full major scale is used here. Most of the pieces employ voices and instruments. Again, progress is logical but 112 pages of C major is a daunting prospect!
Volume 3 – Major: Dominant and Subdominant Triads
Three chords are explored thoroughly, mostly in C major. There are some attractive pieces for smaller groupings, including duets for recorder and timpani. Songs and purely instrumental items are intermixed freely.
Volume 4 – Minor: Drone Bass Triads
More variety is found in this volume, with the Aeolian, Dorian and Phrygian modes being used in turn. Interesting rhythmic groupings and less common time

signatures such as 5/4 offer fresh challenges. The instrumentation ranges from two glockenspiels to a veritable orchestra of 'Orff' instruments with recorders in eight parts and voices in three parts added.

Volume 5 – Minor: Dominant and Subdominant Triads
This is a wonderfully varied collection of pieces for instruments and/or voices, most of which would tax a school choir or orchestra, let alone average classes of children.

Russell-Smith, G., 'The Russell-Smith Method' (E.M.I.)

Book 1: *Let's Explore Music*
Book 2: *Further Afield*
Book 3: *New Horizons*
Book 4: *The Complete Explorer*

This series has much to commend it. A teacher's handbook serves as a guide to the complex but generally well-ordered mixture of glockenspiel and recorder playing and singing. There is a pupil's book and a teacher's accompaniment book at each level. The scheme is built around precepts of the Kodály Method and Orff-Schulwerk. A premium is placed upon the learning of notation, the early stages of the work proceeding at a pace which should produce success in this area. Later on, the progress is unrealistically rapid. Unlike Orff-Schulwerk and the Kodály Method, which have strong idiomatic roots, this course is somewhat uncertain in style. Mr Russell-Smith's avowed distaste both for creative processes and for the use of pop music in class seems to have left him within a stylistic limbo. Nevertheless, there is plenty to work at and the requirements of the course in no way preclude teachers from using other materials alongside.

Pop and rock music

Vulliamy, G. and Lee, E. (eds.), *Pop Music in School, New Edition* (Cambridge University Press, 1980)

The whole of this book is concerned with the topic of pop music but only parts of it are of direct relevance to schoolwork. Of those parts, Piers Spencer's contributions get to the heart of the problems of children playing and composing in pop or Blues style. He demonstrates how the work can grow from simple ostinati (or riffs) into elaborate and lengthy compositions. Similarly, he shows how the activity can be suited to full classes, smaller groups or individuals. There is sufficient information for music teachers to follow his processes in their own classrooms with confidence. The bibliography is extensive but offers few titles specifically about this kind of work in schools.

Vulliamy, G. and Lee, E. (eds.), *Pop, Rock and Ethnic Music in School* (Cambridge University Press, 1982)

This follow-up to *Pop Music in School* contains much of relevance to music teachers. The four main sections entitled 'Classroom work', 'Aspects of technique', 'Ethnic musical styles' and 'Alternatives' cover the subject matter from the viewpoint of the music teacher. There is a refreshing absence of dry academic discussion. Of special interest are the contributions from John Cromer, Michael Burnett and Piers Spencer, all of which provide practical advice for teachers.

Paton, R., *MultiTracks 1: Making Beat Music* (Educational Productions Ltd in collaboration with Chappell & Co.)
1. *Creating Rock* 2. *Playing the Blues* 3. *How to write a Pop Number* 4. *Turning on to Progressive*

Each section of this package consists of a cassette tape, a book of teacher's notes and three workcards. The tape guides groups of pupils through processes which will lead to understanding and performing skill in each area. The work is wholly practical, the taped voice emphasising periodically that now is the time to switch off and to start playing and singing. The four sections form a complete course of work and are bought as a single package. In many ways this teaching programme is well geared to schools. For instance, kazoos, glockenspiels and other classroom instruments are pressed into service. Even a drumkit is not essential. However, the pace of work is fast, even for qualified 'classical' musicians, and some of the ideas being put across are highly sophisticated. It would be best used as a stimulus for smaller groups of older children and for pupils who are already well motivated.

Classroom orchestra

Winters, G., *Musical Instruments in the Classroom* (Longman, 1967)
Winters, G., *An Introduction to Group Music Making. A Practical Guide for the Non-specialist* (Chappell & Co., 1967)

Despite its age, *Musical Instruments in the Classroom* is still a most useful little book. It discusses several aspects of instrumental work, but is a little weak in matters of educational progression. The skills of imitation, improvisation, ostinato work, basic chord work and so on are clearly expounded but not linked together in any obvious way. There are helpful chapters on song accompaniments and group ensemble work.

Mr Winters' other book covers much the same ground, linking the skills to various Chappell publications.

Salaman, W., *Class in Concert, Grades A, B and C* (Middle Eight Music)
Salaman, W., *Class in Concert Encore!* (Middle Eight Music)

Class in Concert is a graded scheme consisting of sixteen pieces for ensembles made up of classroom instruments, guitar and orchestral instruments. There is an optional piano part. The music can be played on classroom instruments only, if preferred. Musical literacy and playing skills are developed throughout the three grades. The recorder part is confined to the left hand notes throughout Grades A and B. The packs include a teacher's score and twenty-six separate parts for the pupils' use. *Class in Concert Encore!* provides supplementary material to *Class in Concert*. It contains twelve pieces which cover the same areas of music reading and playing technique.

Salaman, W., *Concert Starters* (Middle Eight Music)

This is a set of six very simple original pieces for classroom instruments playing together. The recorder part employs the notes B, A and G only in the first four pieces, C and D only in the final two. There is a teacher's score and a set of parts. It is well suited to less able children.

Brace, G., *Something to Play* (Cambridge University Press)

This collection contains fourteen items, mostly presented in duet form and all playable on a variety of instruments. The musical style is imaginatively varied and the compiler makes suggestions for obtaining tonal contrasts and for incorporating unskilled players into the classroom ensemble. Even so, the less able children can encounter problems and the presence of a few expert instrumentalists is vital for successful results. The book might best be used for supplementary rather than introductory work.

Salaman, W., *DuoKits 1–6* (Middle Eight Music)

Though each one of the thirty-four pieces which make up the six kits is in two parts, all are playable on almost any combination of instruments. A set of twenty parts in the treble and bass clefs and for instruments in B flat allows recorders to play with double basses, xylophones with euphoniums. The music can be set as practical homework for two players living near to each other or used in a full class of thirty, playing as a classroom orchestra. The teacher's book contains a score of all the versions alongside an optional piano part. The music is graded throughout.

Orff, C. and Keetman, G., *Music for Children, Vols. 1–5* (Schott)

Many of these pieces can be adapted for use in a classroom orchestra. For details, see above.

Kodály, Z., *Tricinia* (Boosey & Hawkes)

These trios, which form a section of the materials for the *Kodály Choral Method* (see above, p.101), are suitable for more advanced instrumentalists and could provide the basis for small group work.

Chapter 6 Inventive music-making in the classroom

Paynter, J. and Aston, P., *Sound and Silence* (Cambridge University Press, 1970)

This was not the first book to suggest inventive activities in music lessons, but it was, and still is, regarded as the most important influence in the field. The authors are at pains to point out that the book is not a text to be followed slavishly, nor is it a Method. Nevertheless, many of the thirty-six projects have assumed a certain sanctity over the years which has turned their original purpose upside down. What was intended as a stimulus for imaginative thought for teachers has become a substitute for it! Maybe this serves to show how sensible and durable most of the ideas are. The projects are presented in a logical manner and a record illustrating the work is available also.

Paynter, J., *Music in the Secondary School Curriculum – trends and developments in class music teaching* (Cambridge University Press, 1982)

This is a more far-reaching book than *Sound and Silence*. Its publication marks the completion of the Schools Council Project of the same title, much of whose material and philosophy is included. Section 4, 'Creativity and the music curriculum', tackles again the issues raised by musical invention. Paynter argues that many of the non-inventive activities such as instrumental performance, singing and listening should be viewed as being creative. He discusses aspects of work in the music classroom ranging from the underlying rationale for music's presence in schools to problems of accommodation. Perhaps the most stimulating parts of the book are those which discuss children's musical inventiveness and the techniques for harnessing it, though again, a formal 'course' in creative work is neither offered nor proposed.

Paynter, J., 'All Kinds of Music' (Oxford University Press)

1. *Voices*　　2. *Moods and Messages*　　3. *Sound Machines*　　4. *Sound Patterns*

These classroom materials consist of a pupil's book and a recording for each stage plus a vital book of 'teacher's notes' which offer eloquent argument for placing greater emphasis upon creative activities in class and provide helpful advice on the use of the pupil's books and recordings. *Voices* includes songs of all sorts together with material to be used in less (sometimes much less) traditional ways. The apparently strange choice of pitch for the songs is explained in the teacher's notes. *Moods and Messages* contains some exciting suggestions for inventive work like the construction of mock-television commercials and the preparation of scores for film sequences. There is an entertaining section on the tin whistle with playing instructions included. *Sound Machines* explores musical instruments of all kinds. Western orchestral instruments form only part of this lightning guided tour. There are playing instructions for some of them and the tin whistle lessons continue. *Sound Patterns* examines the structures which underlie all music. These range from two-note riffs to dodecaphony, from fugues to composing with tape recorders. Not all of the forms are explained fully, but this linking of structure in music to its *sound* provides a healthy springboard for compositional work.

There are other books and materials relevant to this kind of work in the classroom. Some of the ideas offered will suit only the most adventurous of teachers. A selection of titles is given below.

Schafer, M., *Ear Cleaning* (Universal, 1969)
Schafer, M., *The New Soundscape* (Universal, 1969)
Dennis, B., *Projects in Sound* (Universal, 1975)
Self, G., *Make a New Sound* (Universal, 1976)

Chapter 7 Listening activities in the classroom

Fiske, R., *Score Reading* (Oxford University Press)
1. *Orchestration*   2. *Musical Form*   3. *Concertos*   4. *Oratorios*

These books provide a firm foundation for score-reading activities in class. The compiler is well aware of the implications of such work and provides useful information always relevant to the music being studied. Book 1, *Orchestration*, is the most pedagogic of the four, introducing the pupils to the sounds of orchestral instruments and the skills of following a score concurrently. A little supplementary material is needed at certain stages. The other books contain more music and less commentary. The choice of music examples is unadventurous. Maybe the laws of copyright have prevented the inclusion of more recent twentieth-century works.

Fawcett, B., *Listening and Writing, a Music Workbook* (Harrap)

Consisting of a teacher's book, a pupil's book and a cassette tape, *Listening and Writing* provides ample opportunity for music teachers to meet the author's stated aims: to encourage active and intelligent listening, to link aural training with real musical experience and to develop a wide range of aural skills. Thirty short musical examples, ranging from Bach to Britten, are provided both on the tape and in the books. The pupils arrive at their answers through careful listening, the skills required varying from the elementary to the very advanced. The introduction to the teacher's book must be absorbed thoroughly if the work is to be pitched at an appropriate level at all times. Complete works are not offered, but the tuneful extracts might serve to stimulate more extended listening at a later stage.

Chapter 8 Living school music

The Arts in Schools (Calouste Gulbenkian Foundation, 1982)

This book is a report of an Inquiry into the principles, practice and provision of the arts in schools. For many people, it could act as a guiding light through the labyrinth of complex argument and thought in the area. Against a background of solid factual information, an immensely convincing rationale for the arts in education is given. For music teachers, two vital premises must be established if their subject is to retain credibility. The first is that aesthetic education is as vital as any other branch of schooling while the second is that music as a school subject is an essential part of aesthetic education. This book can leave one in no doubt that both premises are fully tenable.

Ross, M. (ed.), *The Aesthetic Imperative* (Pergamon, 1981)

A disparity of style and viewpoint is clearly evident here, as one might expect in a collection of conference papers, which is what the book consists of. Some of the language used is convoluted and far removed from the realities of the classroom.

However, a few contributions are splendidly down to earth and should help readers to establish their own foundations for the teaching of aesthetic subjects. Malcolm Ross' first chapter, and the contributions from Ernest Goodman, Ben Bradnack and Harry Rée are particularly recommended.